Contents

Chapter 1

The 2010 general election: what happened to FPTP?

Exam success

The up-to-date facts, examples and arguments in this chapter will help you to produce good-quality answers in your AS unit tests in the following areas of the specifications:

Edexcel	AQA	OCR
Unit 1	**Unit 1**	**Unit F851**
Elections	Electoral systems	Political parties
	Political parties	Electoral systems and referenda

Context

The general election of 6 May was extraordinary in that it resulted in no party winning overall control of the House of Commons, and the emergence of a coalition government. This outcome ended the certainty that the first-past-the-post system always produces an outright winner. It may also be the last general election to be fought using this system as there will be a referendum on a change to the Alternative Vote system in 2011. The political and economic circumstances of the election were also unusual: the Labour government had become very unpopular, especially its leader, Gordon Brown, and the UK was teetering on the edge of a serious economic recession. Despite this, neither of the two main opposition parties had made significant headway in opinion polls. The final piece of the jigsaw was the emergence of Liberal Democrat leader Nick Clegg as a serious political figure. It was, therefore, hardly surprising that something unusual should happen.

This chapter considers the impact of the general election result on the first-past-the-post electoral system and the party system. In doing so, it answers the following questions:

- Did the first-past-the-post electoral system operate 'normally'?
- To what extent was the result unusual?
- Does the outcome mark the end of the two-party system?
- Is the UK a natural two-party system?

Was the 2010 result 'normal'?

Table 1.1 Results of the 2010 general election

Party	Number of seats	% of votes	% of seats
Conservative	307	36.1	47.5
Labour	258	29.0	39.9
Liberal Democrat	57	23.0	8.8
Northern Ireland parties*	17	1.7	2.6
Scottish National Party*	6	1.7	0.9
Plaid Cymru*	3	0.6	0.5
Green Party	1	1.0	0.2
Others	0	6.9	0.0

Source: BBC.

* These are regional parties and the percentages are therefore distorted as they only offer candidates in their own region. For the purposes of analysis, they should be ignored.

Yes, it was 'normal'

Many features of the 2010 outcome were predictable and in line with past results. Among them are the following:

■ The Liberal Democrats were hugely discriminated against. They won 23.0% of the votes (a small one-percentage increase since the last election in 2005) but only 8.8% of the seats. In fact, their disadvantage actually grew in 2010 because they attracted more votes but fewer seats.

■ Labour and the Conservatives between them won their 'normal' proportion of the seats in the House of Commons. This was 86.9%, very similar to the elections of 1997, 2001 and 2005 (see Table 1.2 on p. 4).

■ The smaller parties fared badly with only one — the Greens — winning a seat. The UK Independence Party (UKIP) won 3.1% of the national votes but did not win a single seat. The nationalist and Northern Ireland parties did win seats, but this was because they enjoy strong regional support.

■ The Labour Party did disproportionately well. It achieved 29.0% of the national vote and this converted into 39.9% of the seats.

■ The turnout was at a normal level. At just over 65%, it lay between the low levels of around 60% in 2001 and 2005 and the higher levels which used to be seen — between 70 and 75%. We cannot use the level of turnout to explain the unusual outcome.

■ The value of votes for the three main parties remained unequal. If we calculate the number of votes per seat for each of them (by taking the total number of votes cast for each party nationally and dividing this by the number of seats won), we find the following results:

– Conservatives: 34,370 votes per seat won.

– Labour: 33,370 votes per seat won.

– Liberal Democrat: 119,944 votes per seat won.

We can see that there was nearly equality between the value of votes for the two main parties, but votes for Liberal Democrat candidates were of considerably less value. This is normal in UK general elections.

No, it was unusual

Despite these traditional outcomes, 2010 was indeed a very different election. In particular, the following features were interestingly different:

- The disadvantage suffered by the Conservatives was less pronounced. We have seen above that the value of a vote for the Conservatives was of roughly equal value to a vote for Labour.
- A minor party managed to win a parliamentary seat. Caroline Lucas, leader of the Green Party, won the seat at Brighton Pavilion. This was the result of a particularly successful campaign in which the party put a huge amount of resources into its only winnable seat. Ms Lucas was an impressive, well-known individual and Brighton is an unusual seat with an extremely varied electorate. Nevertheless, it was something of a breakthrough.
- There was a significant fall in the proportion of the national vote won by the two parties. Between 1979 and 2005, the two main parties won between 70 and 80% of the national vote. In 2010, this proportion fell to just over 65%. However, this change was not translated into the distribution of seats won. This remained dominated by the Conservatives and Labour together. These trends are shown in Table 1.2 (p. 4).

Box 1.1 The 'normal' view of FPTP

The traditional view of the first-past-the-post electoral system is that it works as follows:

- It discriminates against the smaller parties because they are unable to win any constituencies. It requires at least 30% of the total vote in a constituency (usually more) to win the seat — minor parties cannot achieve this.
- It discriminates against the Liberal Democrats because they are unable to concentrate enough support in most constituencies to win them. In other words, the Liberal Democrats may finish second in many constituencies, but this does them no good in terms of winning seats. They can only win seats in regions where they do have concentrated support, such as southwest England, or where there are special circumstances such as seats contested by nationally well-known figures like Nick Clegg or Vince Cable.
- It discriminates in favour of the Labour Party. This is because Labour has more concentrated support and so has a large number of seats where the party is bound to win. These are mostly traditional industrial areas or places where there are high levels of poverty and deprivation. Northern England is the prime example.
- It discriminates slightly against the Conservatives because their support is more dispersed than Labour, which means they suffer from the same problem as the Liberal Democrats. However, the Conservatives do have concentrated support in the south of England and thus win many seats there.

- The most unusual outcome of the election was of course the fact that no single party won an overall majority in the House of Commons. This was the first time this had happened since February 1974.

An assessment of first-past-the-post in 2010

The clear conclusion of this analysis has to be that the basic operation and impact of the first-past-the-post electoral system was little changed in 2010. True, the outcome was remarkable — a hung or 'balanced' parliament and the first coalition government in the UK since 1945 (bear in mind that coalition governments have been seen in recent years in the devolved administrations in Scotland and Wales) — but first-past-the-post threw up most of the normal features of a general election. What occurred that was different was that the arithmetic happened to add up to no overall majority. Had Labour's vote collapsed a little more than it did, Britain would have seen a Conservative government with a working majority in the House of Commons. The Liberal Democrats did not make an electoral breakthrough and smaller parties remain insignificant. The advantage enjoyed by the two main parties remained crucial.

British politics changed dramatically, therefore, in May 2010, but we cannot look to any change in the first-past-the-post system for an explanation.

Is this the end of the two-party system?

Before this question can be answered, the phrase 'two-party system' needs to be defined. In general terms, it can be viewed thus:
- The two main parties dominate voting in general elections.
- The two main parties win the majority of seats in the House of Commons.
- Only one of the two main parties realistically can form a government.
- The political agenda, including both consensus and conflict, is determined by the two parties.

Table 1.2 Proportion of seats and votes won by Labour and the Conservatives at general elections, 1979–2010

Year	% seats won by Labour and Conservatives together	% votes won by Labour and Conservatives together
1979	95.8	80.8
1983	93.3	70.0
1987	93.0	73.0
1992	93.2	76.3
1997	88.4	73.9
2001	87.8	72.4
2005	85.6	73.9
2010	86.9	65.1

Source: BBC.

- The business of government and parliament is controlled by the two main parties.

It is important to look first at the long-term trends. Table 1.2 shows the extent to which the two main parties have dominated elections since 1979.

Table 1.2 shows that there has been a long-term change in the pattern of voting and the distribution of seats. The proportion of seats won by Labour and the Conservatives has been gradually declining, though this is far from conclusive. The proportion of votes won by the two main parties did decline significantly in 2010, but this may have been a 'blip', a product of a deep disillusionment with party politics. We have to remind ourselves of the context of the 2010 election. It came after the 'credit crunch' and was overshadowed by the spectre of recession and public sector debt. It also followed the MPs' expenses scandal, which caused a good deal of unease about the role of the parties.

The state of the two-party system can now be analysed in the light of the 2010 election.

Yes, the two-party system has declined

- The most important evidence is, of course, the failure of either of the two parties to win an overall majority.
- As is clear from the above analysis, the two parties' shares of the national vote have declined significantly.
- Coalition government means that three, rather than two, parties play an important role in the political agenda. There are a number of issues which are on that agenda because the Liberal Democrats now share power with the Conservatives. Among such issues are: whether the electoral system should be reformed, whether the Trident nuclear missile system should be renewed at great cost, how the welfare benefit system should be overhauled, how higher education should be funded and the future of nuclear energy in the UK.
- The televised leadership debates which occurred during the election campaign introduced the notion of three key political leaders, rather than two. Nick Clegg's impact was considerable and made coalition politics more credible.

No, the two-party system has not declined

- The Liberal Democrats made an electoral breakthrough in 1997, but this was not sustained, so much so that Liberal Democrat representation in the House of Commons fell in 2010.
- None of the smaller parties made any significant headway in 2010. It had been thought that UKIP, especially, would benefit from public disillusionment with national politics, but the party did not come near to winning a single seat, though its share of the vote did rise.

- Although coalition politics appears to suggest that three-party politics has emerged, it can be argued that this is merely two-party politics by another name. Certainly, the coalition behaves largely as if it were a single party. This means that the traditional characteristics of adversarial, government-versus-opposition politics have persisted.

What is the future of two-party politics?

One scenario suggests that two-party politics will reassert itself. This analysis is underpinned by the idea that Britain is, somehow, 'naturally' a two-party system, that it is 'organic' and so will always persist. More specifically, a series of events could occur which would despatch the Liberal Democrats back into the political wilderness. These events might include:

- The referendum on the Alternative Vote (AV) might result in a 'no' vote, thus reducing the chances of the Liberal Democrats making further electoral breakthroughs.
- Even if Britain does adopt AV, it might not result in a marked increase in the number of seats won by Liberal Democrats as their supporters hope.
- The Liberal Democrats' reputation might be destroyed by their cooperation with the Conservative Party. The fact that major cuts in public expenditure are now occurring may be seen as partly the responsibility of the Liberal Democrats. It may also be that the party fails to force the Conservatives into major concessions (for example, over higher education tuition fees or defence expenditure) and so will be viewed as ineffective. Put another way, the Liberal Democrats may lose their progressive 'edge' and so lose much of their traditional support.
- The general experience of coalition politics may turn out to be a bad one, in which case the electorate will become reluctant to support a third party in large numbers.

Another scenario is, however, more optimistic for the Liberal Democrats and other smaller parties. This suggests that a change in the electoral system would be decisive, that people will grow to support the idea of coalition politics where one party is no longer able to dominate the political agenda and that it will be clear that the Liberal Democrats have had a decisive influence over the Conservatives. It may be that the Liberal Democrats will join with Labour in future, but it would still spell the end of the two-party system. Furthermore, a Labour/Lib Dem coalition would be more likely to make a radical change to a more proportional electoral system. The introduction of proportional representation for general elections would almost certainly end two-party domination for the foreseeable future.

Summary

The 2010 general election can be seen as both 'normal' and 'abnormal'. It was normal in its general operation, but abnormal in terms of its outcome. For the time being, two-party politics in the UK is suspended. Whether it will return soon depends on whether the electoral system is reformed and/or whether one of the two main parties can achieve a dominant position by capturing a significantly increased share of the popular vote.

Exam focus

To consolidate your knowledge of this chapter, answer the following questions:

1 Account for the result of the 2010 general election.
2 Did the 2010 general election spell the end of two-party politics in the UK?
3 In what ways does the 2010 general election provide evidence to support reform of the electoral system?
4 Can the British system now be accurately described as 'three-party politics'?

Chapter 2

TV debates: the game changer of the campaign?

Exam success

The up-to-date facts, examples and arguments in this chapter will help you to produce good-quality answers in your AS unit tests in the following areas of the specifications:

Edexcel	AQA	OCR
Unit 1	**Unit 1**	**Unit F851**
Elections	Participation and voting behaviour	UK parliamentary elections Voting behaviour in the UK

Context

On 21 December 2009, the BBC confirmed that an agreement had been struck to hold three televised debates between the leaders of the main UK political parties during the 2010 general election campaign. Though this was not the first time that such a spectacle had been proposed, earlier plans for such set-piece events had always fallen through as a result of either the reluctance of one or more of the leaders to participate, or the failure of the main television broadcasters to settle on a mutually agreeable format. By the end of 2009, however, both obstacles appeared to have been overcome, with Gordon Brown, David Cameron and Nick Clegg all signing up to the project and the three main UK television providers — ITV, Sky and the BBC — agreeing a common format for a series of three debates, one per broadcaster (see Box 2.1).

This chapter considers the extent to which the three televised debates held in April 2010 influenced the course of the general election campaign, as well as addressing the broader question of whether such broadcasts enhance or detract from the democratic process. In doing so, it answers the following questions:

- Did the televised debates improve the Lib Dems' electoral prospects?
- Did the televised debates enhance Nick Clegg's reputation and/or public confidence in his party?
- Do such televised debates enhance democracy?

Did the debates improve the Lib Dems' electoral prospects?

Precisely what prompted such a turnaround with regard to televised debates is open to question. Previously, Gordon Brown and his predecessor as prime minister, Tony Blair, had maintained that Prime Minister's Questions and other

Box 2.1 Details of the agreement on televised leader debates

- Three 'prime ministerial debates' to be held during the election campaign itself
- The first debate on ITV, the second on Sky and the third on the BBC
- Each debate to be chaired by a high-profile host — Alastair Stewart for ITV, Adam Boulton for Sky and David Dimbleby for the BBC

such events gave the public ample opportunity to see the premier addressing the topical issues of the day. Why, it was argued, should we go down the US route of personalised head-to-head debates between the party leaders, when UK voters are casting their ballots not directly for the prime minister but for their constituency MP? In a sense, the U-turn on televised debates must be seen in the context both of the battering that public confidence in politicians took over MPs' expenses, and of the ongoing concern over falling levels of participation in formal politics, specifically, electoral turnout at the 2001 and 2005 general elections. As the Liberal Democrat leader Nick Clegg remarked on BBC Online, 'after a terrible year for politicians, these debates will be an opportunity to start re-engaging people with politics... I hope an open, honest and vigorous debate will encourage more people to have their say at the ballot box.'

The Lib Dems had always pushed for such debates. They clearly felt that they would benefit from the additional exposure gained, not least because their efforts to campaign on an equal footing with the two main parties had always been hindered by issues of unequal funding and media access.

The ICM poll completed on 11 April, four days before the first televised debate, showed the Lib Dems trailing on 20%, well behind Labour (on 31%) and the Conservatives (on 37%). This was broadly in line with the 11 previous ICM polls taken since July 2009, where support for the party had always been between 18% and 23%. In the wake of the first televised debate, however, support for the Lib Dems rose to 24%, with 51% believing that the Lib Dem leader had 'won' the opening head-to-head between the leaders of the three main parties. Indeed, 29% felt that Clegg would make the best prime minister (the same number that favoured Cameron).

Though support for the two main parties recovered in the wake of the second and third debates (see Table 2.1), it was still widely anticipated that the Lib Dems would emerge on election night with more MPs than the 62 returned at the 2005 general election.

Did the Lib Dems perform better because of the debates?

'What if' questions are notoriously hard to answer. It is indeed difficult to know just 'what might have been' had the televised debates not taken place.

Table 2.1 Who won the three televised debates?

	Focus of debate	Who won?		
		Brown	Cameron	Clegg
First debate (ITV, 15 April)	Domestic affairs	19%	20%	51%
Second debate (BSkyB, 22 April)	International affairs	29%	29%	33%
Third debate (BBC, 29 April)	Economic affairs	29%	35%	27%

Source: ICM instant polling for the Guardian, as reported in the Guardian on 16, 23 and 30 April.

Ahead of the election, it was widely felt that the Lib Dem vote would be squeezed in a battle between a Labour Party fighting to stay in office and defend its legacy, and a Conservative Party 'detoxified' and resurgent under the leadership of David Cameron. It should also be remembered that the Lib Dems' record haul of seats in 2005 had been secured, at least in part, as a result of the backlash against Labour's decision to take the country to war in Iraq, the Lib Dems having been the only one of the three main UK parties to oppose the deployment.

All of this accepted, it is possible to identify a number of points that could reasonably be offered in support of each side of the argument identified.

Yes, they performed better

- While it was widely anticipated that the Lib Dem vote would be squeezed, the party actually increased its share of the vote from 22% in 2005 to 23% in 2010, securing only 1.8 million votes fewer than Labour (6.8 million to Labour's 8.6 million).
- This final percentage share of the vote was significantly higher than that reported in the final opinion polls taken in the run-up to the first debate. Indeed, it was the highest share of the vote for the third party since the 1983 general election, when the SDP-Liberal Alliance polled 25.4%.
- It should be remembered that even after the first debate, only around 24% of those polled by ICM said that they intended to vote Lib Dem. A return of 23% should not, therefore, be seen as a failure.
- Though the Lib Dems won fewer seats in 2010 than in 2005 (down five at 57), this disappointing return resulted largely from the quirks of the simple plurality system employed, as opposed to any decline in support. This is demonstrated, for example, by the fact that the Lib Dems came second in 243 constituencies.

No, they did not perform better

- The Lib Dems only achieved a marginal increase in their share of the popular vote (up from 22% in 2005 to 23% in 2010) in spite of the apparent surge in support for the party in the wake of the first debate.
- Despite the televised debates, the Lib Dems returned fewer MPs in 2010 than in 2005.

- Although it was generally agreed that the Labour leader Gordon Brown performed poorly against Nick Clegg, particularly in the first two debates, the Lib Dems only captured five Labour seats. Indeed, even with the Labour Party in apparent disarray, the Lib Dems still won 201 seats fewer than Labour.
- 27 of the 57 seats won by the Lib Dems appear in the list of the top 200 with smallest majorities, i.e. they were lucky to win as many seats as they did.

Whatever happened to the 'Lib Dem surge'?

The simple answer to this question, as we have seen, is that the first televised debate resulted in a 'Nick Clegg surge' as opposed to a 'Lib Dem surge'. Indeed, while the party did enjoy a 'bounce' in the polls in the wake of the first debate on 15 April, it was the Lib Dem leader and not his party's policies that emerged victorious. Although Clegg had worked hard to reposition the Lib Dems in many areas of policy ahead of the election (see *UK Government and Politics Annual Survey 2010*), the broader public still viewed many of the party's policies with a degree of suspicion. This was true, for example, of the Lib Dem approach to managing immigration — a policy on which the Lib Dem leader came under heavy fire during the second televised debate and one that took centre stage in the media post-mortem that followed the election itself.

Did the debates enhance Clegg's reputation and/or confidence in his party?

While it is tempting to focus on the Lib Dems' failure to capitalise on the brief surge in the polls that followed the first debate by winning more seats in the Commons, such an approach runs the risk of missing the 'bigger picture'. As stated earlier, the surge was far more about public perceptions of the Lib Dem leader, Nick Clegg, than it was about voting intentions, and it is perhaps in this light that we should answer the question of whether or not the televised debates were a 'game changer'. In short, the debates and the broader campaign itself were about more than simply winning votes and seats. They were about making the broader public (and perhaps also senior figures within the other main parties) see the Lib Dems as a 'party of government' — a credible alternative to the 'big two', or at least a credible coalition partner for one or the other.

Prior to the debates, the public perception of the Lib Dem leader had been shaped largely by reporting of his sexual conquests in earlier life (for which he briefly earned the media moniker 'Cleggover') or from seeing Clegg struggling to make himself heard over the heckling of Labour and Conservative back-benchers at Prime Minister's Questions. It was significant, therefore, that the regulations governing the televised debates — not least the rules limiting audience participation — meant that Clegg was able to speak, uninterrupted, for extended periods.

'I agree with Nick'

Clegg's credibility was also enhanced by the way in which his fellow party leaders, in particular Gordon Brown, appeared to court his support in the first debate by publicly approving the positions adopted by the Lib Dem leader. If one had to pick a single phrase that summed up the reporting of that first debate more than any other, it would have to be 'I agree with Nick'. Though that precise phrase was in fact only used twice over the course of the 90-minute broadcast (on both occasions by Gordon Brown), it appeared to sum up the broad approach taken by both the incumbent prime minister and, to a lesser extent, David Cameron, towards the Lib Dem leader. Brown, in particular, appeared keen to align himself with Clegg at every opportunity (see Box 2.2).

Box 2.2	Phrases used by Gordon Brown towards Nick Clegg in the first televised debate

- 'I agree with Nick...' (used twice)
- '...where Nick and I agree...'
- 'As Nick said...'
- '...which is what Nick has referred to...'
- 'I don't think that David will support us on this, but I hope Nick will...'

Source: full transcript of the first televised debate.

The 'Clegg surge' that resulted, in part, from Brown's approach in the first debate prompted the Labour leader to adopt a rather different line in the second debate broadcast on Sky. While the Sky debate saw the prime minister using the phrase 'Nick, you're right' at one point, Brown's general approach was to seek to highlight the differences (as opposed to the similarities) between his position and that of the Lib Dem leader (see Box 2.3) — an approach that was carried through to the third debate. By that stage, however, the damage had largely been done.

Box 2.3	Phrases used by Gordon Brown towards Nick Clegg in the second televised debate

- 'Let's be honest, and Nick didn't say this.'
- 'Nick, you leave us weak.'
- 'Nick is a risk to our security with his nuclear weapons policy.'
- 'I say to you, Nick, get real, get real, get real.'
- 'I'm very worried about Nick's policy.'

Source: full transcript of the second televised debate.

Do televised debates enhance democracy?

Yes, they do

- Such televised debates provide an additional avenue for political participation. More than 9 million people watched the first debate, with around 4 million watching the second and well over 8 million watching the third.
- The radio phone-ins, newspaper articles and other media coverage that came in the wake of each debate provided additional opportunities for voters to engage with the general election campaign.
- The debate gave equal voice to the Lib Dems, a party often disadvantaged by its relative lack of campaign finance and limited media access.
- The debates gave an opportunity for selected audience members to quiz the party leaders on some of the detail behind their manifesto pledges.

No, they do not

- While televised debates make some sense in US presidential elections, where voters are electing a singular (or 'unitary') executive, they make little sense in the UK where voters are instead choosing their constituency MP.
- The quality of democratic participation involved in watching television is, at best, limited.
- The debates gave the Lib Dems more exposure than could be justified either by the party's performance at earlier elections or by the number of seats they ultimately won in 2010.
- Other parties such as the SNP, Plaid Cymru and UKIP were excluded from the three debates. The SNP argued that this put them at a distinct disadvantage in parliamentary contests north of the border.
- The separate Scottish and Welsh debates featured the leaders of the SNP (Alex Salmond) and Plaid Cymru (Ieuan Jones) respectively, but neither had the opportunity to go toe-to-toe with Brown, Cameron and Clegg.

Summary

- While the three televised debates did not bring the significant electoral gains for the Lib Dems that had been anticipated, they clearly enhanced Nick Clegg's reputation and credibility.
- This may have made it easier for the Conservatives to conclude a coalition deal with the Lib Dems when faced with the hung (or 'balanced') parliament that resulted from the 2010 general election.
- While the debates provided a point of interest in the campaign and an additional avenue for political participation, they appeared somewhat at odds with a parliamentary system under which citizens vote not for their preferred prime minister but for their constituency MP.
- The decision to exclude smaller parties from the three main debates led to accusations of media bias.

Exam focus

To consolidate your knowledge of this chapter, answer the following questions.

1 Why did the two main party leaders change their minds about televised leaders' debates?
2 Did the Lib Dems perform better than they would have done if there had been no debates?
3 Do televised debates enhance democracy?
4 To what extent were the TV debates 'the game-changer' of the campaign?

Chapter 3

Coalition government: a new way of governing?

Exam success

The up-to-date facts, examples and arguments in this chapter will help you to produce good-quality answers in your AS unit tests in the following areas of the specifications:

Edexcel	AQA	OCR
Unit 1	**Unit 1**	**Unit F851**
Party policies and ideas	Political parties	Political parties
Unit 2	**Unit 2**	**Unit F852**
The prime minister and cabinet	The core executive	The executive

Context

Britain has not had a coalition government since 1945. This is, therefore, completely new territory for those who practise or study politics. It may even be that by the time you are reading this chapter, the coalition will have fallen. In any case the prime minister, cabinet and ministers will all have to seek new ways of governing in the context of coalition government. The doctrine of collective responsibility will have to be modified and it will have to be accepted that the days of totally single-minded, disciplined and unified government may be behind us, for the time being at least.

This chapter considers the ways in which coalition government came about and the nature of its impact on the governing process and its institutions. In doing so, it answers the following questions:

- What arrangements were made in May 2010 in order to facilitate the formation of a coalition government?
- What effect is the coalition government likely to have on the doctrine of collective responsibility?
- How is decision making likely to be conducted in a coalition government?
- What developments might occur in the future with regard to policy agreement and conflict?

> Today we are not just announcing a new government and new ministers. We are announcing a new politics. A new politics where the national interest is more important than party interest. Where cooperation wins out over confrontation. Where compromise, give and take, reasonable, civilised, grown-up behaviour is not a sign of weakness but of strength.

This was how, in May 2010, David Cameron announced the formation of Britain's first coalition government since 1945. Clearly, Cameron and his coalition partner Nick Clegg believed they were heralding a historic and long-term change in the nature of politics. Here we examine these claims in the light of the first few months of the new government.

How is coalition government likely to operate?

Before evaluating the new government, it is useful to examine exactly what coalition government entails.

- Of the 23 **cabinet** positions, five have been taken by Liberal Democrat ministers and the remaining 18 are Conservatives. This seems to be a 'fixed' division of posts, demonstrated by the fact that when Liberal Democrat cabinet minister David Laws resigned following damaging allegations over his MP's expenses claims, he was replaced by another Liberal Democrat to restore the balance between the two parties.
- There is a similar distribution of posts among the 80 or so **junior ministers** who are not in the cabinet.
- The coalition has made and published a formal agreement on all main policies. This constitutes official **coalition policy** and, therefore, government policy.
- Any new policies, not originally envisaged in the coalition agreement of May 2010, must be agreed in cabinet to become **official government policy**. If agreement cannot be reached, the issue cannot become official policy.
- There are some policy issues where there is an **agreement to differ**. This is not government policy until specific decisions are made by the coalition cabinet.
- **Collective government responsibility** applies in the coalition government. This is examined further below.
- The British form of coalition does not mean that the responsibilities of government have been divided up between the parties. All government areas of policy are the responsibility of the coalition government as a whole. Thus, George Osborne, a Conservative, is in charge of economic management as Chancellor of the Exchequer, while Vince Cable, a Liberal Democrat, is Business Secretary, yet this does not imply that the Conservatives control the economy and the Liberal Democrats control business — both the economy and business are to be **governed by the whole cabinet**.

It is clear that this form of coalition (in other parts of the democratic world, coalition governments may operate differently) needs a delicate balance and requires a great deal of cooperation between the two partners. At the centre of this balance lies the doctrine of collective cabinet responsibility (see Box 3.1).

The nature of collective responsibility

This traditional doctrine is made up of the following elements:

- All members of the government, whether in the cabinet or not, must publicly support government policy, as declared by the cabinet.
- If a minister disagrees privately with government policy, he or she must keep his or her opposition private. He or she must not make public statements that challenge government policy.
- If a minister wishes publicly to oppose or question government policy, he or she must resign from the government (and thus return to the backbenches of parliament).
- A minister who disagrees publicly with government policy and does not resign must face dismissal by the prime minister.
- Above all, collective responsibility means that the *whole* government is collectively responsible for all government policy. Theoretically, therefore, the whole government stands or falls together.

How will collective responsibility work?

Clearly coalition government places an enormous strain on collective responsibility. During the general election campaign, the two coalition partners presented different sets of policies and criticised many of each other's policies. Once in government together, however, leading members of each party are expected to support the government as a whole, *including* some policies which they opposed in the election campaign.

Some examples of policies where there were considerable differences in positions between the Conservatives and the Liberal Democrats illustrate the problem:

- At the end of 2010 the issue of higher education tuition fees shook the coalition arrangement to its core. The Liberal Democrat leadership, having made a commitment to oppose fee rises, was forced to abandon its opposition in the interests of coalition unity. In the event there were two junior government resignations by Liberal Democrats (plus one Conservative junior ministerial aide). The five Liberal Democrat cabinet ministers, however, held firm and retained collective responsibility by supporting government policy despite intense public and media pressure to honour their election pledge by voting against the increases.
- The Conservatives supported the proposal to renew the Trident submarine nuclear missile system at enormous cost to the taxpayer in years to come while the Liberal Democrats proposed that Trident should be scrapped or at least seriously curtailed.
- The Conservatives support the expansion of the nuclear energy programme. The Liberal Democrats oppose this, preferring other forms of renewable or 'clean' energy generation.

- In more general terms, the Liberal Democrats favour a more 'progressive' tax system than the Conservatives. Essentially this means that the Liberal Democrats believe a higher proportion of the tax burden should fall on the well-off. Conservatives argue that excessively taxing the rich would be a disincentive to enterprise and wealth creation and thus would damage the economy in the long term.

There are, of course, other areas of disagreement and more will arise as time goes by, but these four issues are prime examples of potential difficulties.

How will these problems be solved?

Ways have to be found to solve these problems while preserving the basic principle of collective responsibility. We can view the proposed arrangements on a five-level scheme.

Level 1 Clearly the ordinary 'grassroots' members (i.e. those who do not hold any elective office) of each party are free to debate and argue over all policies. Thus, at the autumn 2010 conferences of both coalition parties, there was a good deal of debate over whether too many compromises were being made by the party leaders. Such debates may have some influence over the leaderships but are unlikely to be decisive.

Level 2 MPs and peers from the two parties may be 'encouraged' to support coalition policy despite private misgivings, but are still free to speak out if they wish to demonstrate opposition. The party whips will insist that backbench MPs and peers support the coalition government on important parliamentary divisions (that is, votes on legislation or key decisions). There will be some backbench 'revolts', for certain. The question is: how may revolts will there be and how many MPs or peers will join them? Thus, backbench opposition may embarrass the party leaderships but will not threaten the coalition, unless such backbench opposition becomes widespread.

Level 3 Coalition ministers may argue and debate about policy within the private circles of government. Such policy disagreements and negotiations must, however, remain private. This is potentially the most difficult level.

Level 4 Once the coalition cabinet has made and published a decision or a policy, all ministers in the coalition are bound by collective responsibility and must support the policy or decision. The alternative is that they should resign. Ministerial resignations over policy would threaten the very existence of coalition government. It may survive a small number of resignations by junior ministers, but it cannot afford to lose more than one or two cabinet ministers. As we have seen above, this is what happened over the rises in university tuition fees which passed through parliament in December 2010. Two junior Liberal Democrat members of the government resigned (as well as one Conservative) and voted against the measure, but the five Liberal Democrat cabinet ministers supported the coalition policy.

Level 5   Ultimately, if an agreement cannot be reached between the parties on a key issue, the party leaders — Cameron and Clegg — will intervene to try to hammer out a solution between themselves and then seek to carry the cabinet with them.

Compromise, consensus and procrastination

It is likely that coalition politics will include all three of these characteristics. They require some explanation.

Compromise

Compromise implies that a policy is developed which is a mixture between the differing ideas of each of the coalition parties. It involves, in other words, some 'give and take'. The parties will probably continue to disagree, but have made concessions in the national interest and in the interests of the government.

Consensus

Consensus may sound similar but is actually rather different from compromise. This means developing policies *only* upon which both parties already agree. It means, therefore, that policies may be dropped if general agreement cannot be reached.

Procrastination

Procrastination means putting decisions off to a later date. This is a classic political device which is used when a decision is likely to cause a great deal of disagreement and therefore embarrassment to a government.

How will compromise, consensus and procrastination work?

In the early months of the coalition, we can identify examples of all three forms of coalition governing.

Compromise

The most striking example of a policy born out of compromise is the issue of electoral reform. The Conservatives do not favour reform and would prefer to leave first-past-the-post in place for general elections. The Liberal Democrats wish to replace first-past-the-post with proportional representation (PR). The compromise is twofold. First, there will be a referendum on the introduction of the Alternative Vote system (AV) in 2011. AV is a compromise. It reforms the electoral system and can be seen as a 'fairer' system, but it is not full PR. Second, the Conservatives have supported the holding of a referendum and will abide by the result, but they are free to campaign *against* a 'yes' vote for

AV. There is also likely to be a good deal of compromise between the two parties over taxation policy.

There was a hasty compromise to force the rise in university tuition fees through parliament in December 2010. Additional provision was added at the last minute to help students on very low family incomes, thus placating some Liberal Democrat opponents.

Consensus

All three main parties have supported the extension of the academy school programme. There may be disagreements over detail, but there is consensus that the programme is a positive development and the creation of new academies is to be supported. (It should be noted that there is certainly *no* consensus over the creation of 'free schools' to be set up by groups of parents or other community organisations.) A further example of consensus is the principle that front line services in health and education should escape the public expenditure cuts to come.

Procrastination

In September 2010, it was announced that the decision concerning the renewal of the Trident nuclear defence system would be postponed. Thus, the fundamental opposition of the Liberal Democrats to renewal would be sidelined for the time being, while other difficult decisions (mainly on how to deal with the massive level of government debt) are being thrashed out.

Box 3.2 **'Coalition watch'**

How are students to judge the future of coalition government? Two suggestions might help:

- Watch out for the issues similar to the tuition fees conflict which are likely to cause problems for the coalition in the months and years to come. These include:
  - How will policy on banking practice unfold?
  - Will the 2010 spending review, which introduced massive, widespread cuts in public expenditure, cause major areas of dissension among the party leaderships and on the backbenches?
  - In the longer term, the forthcoming 'defence review', which will plan defence policy for years to come, may create fault lines in the coalition.
  - The ways in which welfare benefits are to be reformed, especially unemployment, pensioner and disability benefits, are potentially explosive.
- You can play a 'coalition game'. This entails looking at future major policy decisions and establishing whether they are examples of compromise, consensus or procrastination, as described above.

What is the future of coalition government in the UK?

This can be summed up in one word: **uncertain**. It is possible to envisage either that the coalition will already have fallen by the time this *Annual Survey* is published, or it could endure until 2015 when the next general election is scheduled to take place. The UK has entered unchartered waters. What has happened is that the coalition partners have attempted to synthesise two political features — coalition government and collective responsibility. It is a classic British constitutional compromise. Is it possible to change the way in which politics is carried out in central government and parliament without abandoning the basic principle that government and cabinet are collectively responsible for decision making?

The most dramatic possible scenarios include another election in the next year or two because coalition politics has not worked; the total splitting of the Conservative or Liberal Democrat parties or both; an attempt by the Conservatives to govern as a minority if the Liberal Democrats leave the coalition. As things stand however, the leading members of both coalition parties remain optimistic.

As Vince Cable, the government's Business Secretary and a member of the more radical wing of his party, declared when he spoke at the Liberal Democrat annual party conference in September 2010:

> We will fight the next general elections as an independent force with our options open. Just like 2010. But coalition is the future of politics. It is good for government and good for Britain. We must make sure it is good for the Lib Dems as well.

Summary

The key points considered in this chapter have been:

- Coalition government means that cabinet posts are shared between parties and there must be compromises made to create an agreed policy programme.
- The 'rules' of collective responsibility will have to be modified and weakened.
- Future policy differences will have to be reconciled in cabinet or by the two party leaders.
- Because some policy differences cannot be reconciled, there will have to be many compromises and some decisions will have to be put off altogether.

Exam focus

To consolidate your knowledge of this chapter, answer the following questions:

1 How is the doctrine of collective responsibility affected by the introduction of coalition government?
2 How can Conservatives and Liberal Democrats reconcile policy differences within government?
3 How is cabinet government likely to be affected by coalition politics?

Chapter 4

The coalition agreement: compromise or blueprint for the future?

Exam success

The up-to-date facts, examples and arguments in this chapter will help you to produce good-quality answers in your AS unit tests in the following areas of the specifications:

Edexcel	AQA	OCR
Unit 1	**Unit 1**	**Unit F851**
Party policies and ideas	Political parties	Political parties

Context

The coalition agreement came into force in May 2010. Its first major test was the autumn spending review which introduced swingeing cuts in public expenditure across most areas of government responsibility. This was a potentially divisive event but the coalition held firm and the programme of cuts was met with general approval, or at least acquiescence. The process was eased in November 2010 by the successful passage through parliament of the bill paving the way for a referendum on electoral reform, scheduled for May 2011. Nevertheless, a 'no' vote in May would place additional strain on relations between the Conservatives and the Liberal Democrats. However, the wave of student protests which greeted the announcement of steep rises in higher education tuition fees split the Liberal Democrats. Liberal Democrat ministers were bound by collective responsibility, but MPs were not so constrained and a number joined the opposition over the issue. Despite this, the coalition did survive its first major test when the divisions over rises in university tuition fees did not result in a government defeat in parliament.

This chapter considers the nature of the coalition agreement of May 2010 and evaluates whether it is merely a pragmatic means by which such a coalition could be created or whether it can be considered to be a long-term political programme. In doing so, it answers the following questions:

- What made the coalition agreement possible?
- What are the main terms of the coalition agreement?
- What policy problems may threaten the coalition?
- What compromises had to be made by both parties?
- To what extent is there now consensus between the parties?
- What ideological rifts remain between the coalition partners?

It was an extraordinary achievement for the two coalition partners to have reached a policy agreement within days of the general election of 6 May 2010. In other European countries, where coalition governments are the norm, negotiations can be extremely protracted, but the Conservatives and Liberal Democrats in the UK this year were able to publish a joint policy statement extremely quickly. It is, therefore, immediately clear that there was a great deal of determination to create stable government as soon as possible, especially in view of the need for fast and decisive action to deal with the huge public debt which had been accumulating over several years. It should also be borne in mind that neither party was prepared for such events. The hung parliament was not planned for and, even those who foresaw such a development expected there to be a Labour–Lib Dem coalition rather than an agreement with the Conservatives.

Why was the agreement possible?

This is an important question in view of the fact that this was such a surprising chain of events. We can identify three factors that made the agreement possible:

- The Liberal Democrats saw this as perhaps a once-in-a-lifetime opportunity to share power. This breakthrough would enable them to reform the constitution in such a way that their party would no longer suffer 'discrimination' and so would be able to pursue power in the long term. Having failed to reach agreement with the Labour Party over the weekend after the election, the Liberal Democrats were faced with a choice: should they reject the Conservatives' offer of a partnership and face the possibility of returning to the political wilderness, or should they show willingness to compromise in order to gain a foothold on power?
- David Cameron had shifted the Conservative Party towards the 'centre' of politics by adopting a number of 'liberal' policies. The gulf between the two parties, which had been vast up to 2005, was therefore much narrower than it had been.
- The country was in a precarious economic position. There was the threat of a major economic recession after the 'credit crunch' and there was an urgent need to tackle the huge government deficit. The prospect of a protracted period of political uncertainty could spell economic disaster. This reality concentrated the minds of the two political leaderships.

What are the main elements of the coalition agreement?

When studying the terms of the coalition agreement, it is important to distinguish between *specific* commitments and those which are rather *vague* policies. Table 4.1 does make such distinctions.

Table 4.1 Some key elements of the coalition agreement of May 2010

Firm commitments	General policies and intentions
Banking	**Banking**
■ A 'levy' to be charged to the banks. Its precise nature to be determined. Effectively a 'bank tax' ■ To transfer regulation of the banking system to the Bank of England (away from the Financial Services Authority) ■ To set up a national free financial advice service ■ Britain will not adopt the euro as its currency as long as the coalition government is in office	■ To introduce more competition in banking ■ To introduce measures to ensure more responsible banking and financial practices ■ Controls over excessive bank bonuses
Business	**Business**
■ 25% of public sector contracts to be awarded to small and medium-sized enterprises ■ The Post Office to be allowed to raise capital in private markets	■ A general commitment to cut red tape and over-regulation ■ A general intention to reduce regulation of labour markets, creating more flexibility in employment practices ■ Corporate taxes to be simplified ■ The scale of business taxes to be reviewed
Civil liberties	**Civil liberties**
■ The proposed ID card scheme to be scrapped ■ The DNA records of suspected persons to be kept for a shorter period of time ■ A freedom bill to be passed, though its terms are to be determined	■ Strengthening the Freedom of Information Act ■ A commission to review the European Convention on Human Rights to establish whether a new British version can be adopted ■ Review of anti-terrorism legislation ■ Greater regulation of the use of CCTV ■ To reduce controls on non-violent protest
Communities and local government	**Communities and local government**
■ Referendums to be held in major cities to determine whether there should be an elected mayor ■ Local councils to publish precise details of how taxpayers' money is being spent ■ Council tax to be frozen for at least one year	■ More local democratic control over planning issues ■ Stamp Duty (tax on purchasing houses) to be reviewed ■ Stricter controls over the energy efficiency of new housing

Firm commitments	General policies and intentions
Crime and policing	**Crime and policing**
■ To ban the sale of alcohol products at below cost price ■ Police forces to publish full local crime statistics every month	■ Measures to reduce the amount of administration that police have to do ■ To give local authorities and police greater powers to shut down premises selling alcohol when they create public disorder ■ To review taxation and therefore pricing of alcohol ■ Police forces to be made more publicly accountable ■ Hospitals to be asked to share information about gun and knife crime
Defence	**Defence**
■ Britain to retain a nuclear deterrent ■ Pay allowances for forces on active service to be increased	■ Major savings to be made in defence administration costs ■ Improving conditions for injured servicemen and women
Reducing the financial deficit	**Reducing the financial deficit**
■ Office of Budgetary Responsibility introduced, independent of government, to oversee the reduction of government debt ■ Immediate cuts in public expenditure of £6 billion, to be followed by a spending review for 2011 onwards ■ To cancel the proposed increase on National Insurance payments by employers (so-called 'jobs tax')	■ Rapid movement towards reducing government debt ■ To reduce the number of 'quangos' (quasi-autonomous non-government organisations) ■ To attack the deficit through expenditure reduction rather than by increasing taxes ■ Ensuring that government departments give value for taxpayers' money
Environment	**Environment**
■ To increase the generation of nuclear energy ■ To cancel the third runway for Heathrow airport ■ To increase passenger duties on air travel ■ Opposition to the resumption of commercial whaling ■ A 'Green Investment' bank will be set up to channel funds towards environment-improving projects	■ To introduce more ambitious targets on the creation of renewable energy ■ To encourage more forestry ■ To improve animal welfare ■ To campaign for stricter air quality controls in the EU

Firm commitments	General policies and intentions
Europe	**Europe**
■ Britain will not join the eurozone during the life of the current parliament ■ No transfers of sovereignty to Europe during the current parliament ■ Any future transfer of sovereignty to the EU to be subject to a referendum	■ Support for future enlargement of the European Union ■ Possibility of passing a UK Sovereignty Act to entrench the sovereignty of parliament
Taxation	**Taxation**
■ There will be year-by-year progress towards the development of a £10,000 per annum tax-free allowance ■ Income tax arrangements will give an advantage to married couples ■ The higher-level tax for those earning over £100,000 per annum will be retained	■ The scale of inheritance tax will be reviewed ■ Taxes on businesses to be simplified and, eventually, reduced
Economy	**Economy**
■ Agreement that the government deficit should be eliminated as quickly as is feasible ■ An Office for Budget Responsibility has been set up to prevent future irresponsible spending and borrowing by the government	■ There is a general understanding that, on the whole, free markets and economic competition should be encouraged
Welfare	**Welfare**
■ Health and education to be protected from future government cuts ■ Reductions in welfare benefits to be confined to higher income earners	■ Unspecific commitment to reduce benefit fraud ■ A general commitment to protect pensioners from expenditure cuts
Government and constitution	**Government and constitution**
■ The second chamber to be wholly or substantially elected ■ A referendum to be held on the introduction of AV for general elections ■ Significant savings to be made in all government departments and the abolition of many quangos	■ Greater independence for local government ■ Consideration given to strengthening the protection of human rights

Table 4.1 is not an exhaustive list of coalition policies, but it can be immediately seen that there is a close balance between specific commitments and general policies. In that sense, the agreement is indeed a compromise. Wherever there is a problem between the two parties over a policy, the solution was to publish a very generalised statement of the policy. Whether or not it will be implemented will therefore be the subject of future negotiation.

What are the unresolved issues and policies?

Some policy issues upon which the two coalition parties cannot agree are specified in the agreement. Others are simply not mentioned specifically. These represent the major problem of coalition government: is it advisable to abandon *any* policies that threaten a split, or should the issues be confronted and some kind of compromise reached? The list below identifies the policies where Conservatives and Liberal Democrats do not agree in any sense. The question is: will it be possible to deal with them without bringing the coalition down?

- The main problem has been the proposed increases in tuition fees for universities, with some institutions expecting to charge £9,000 per year. The Liberal Democrats had made a firm commitment to oppose such fee rises. The decision by their leaders, Clegg and Cable included, to support the Conservative plans placed the party in a difficult position, not least because many members represented constituencies in university towns. The revolt by a number of Liberal Democrat MPs was not decisive, but demonstrated how fragile the coalition can be. Even though the coalition survived the vote, the issue is likely to rumble on for some time as the effects of the policy begin to unfold.
- The Conservatives wish to renew the Trident nuclear missile programme at huge cost to the taxpayer over many years. The Liberal Democrats are opposed.
- The Liberal Democrats oppose expansion of nuclear energy while the Conservatives see nuclear energy as one of the solutions to creating a greater reliance on renewable energy.
- It remains unclear how tax policy will unfold. The Liberal Democrats favour a much more progressive tax system (i.e. one that taxes the wealthy at a much higher rate than the poor) than the Conservatives. The coalition has committed itself to raising the starting point for income tax to £10,000 per year, but there remain issues over the extent to which taxes on the rich (e.g. inheritance tax) should be held down.
- The Liberal Democrats, especially Business Secretary Vince Cable, want to see radical reform of the banking system. This contrasts with the Conservatives who are reluctant to alienate the banking community, which may threaten to move the operations abroad.
- Conservatives have declared that they wish to 'wage war' on welfare benefit 'cheats' and, in the words of Chancellor George Osborne, 'choose dependency on welfare as a lifestyle choice' rather than seeking work. Liberal Democrats fear that stricter rules on benefits will disadvantage many who are reliant on welfare through no fault of their own. Reform of the benefits system in general may cause a good deal of tension between the parties.

■ Law and order in general is a potential flashpoint, with Conservatives generally taking a harder line on crime than Liberal Democrats, who favour prevention and rehabilitation over harsh deterrence. That said, both parties have declared opposition to increasing police powers and have declared support for civil liberties above such powers (e.g. ID cards, the DNA database, CCTV surveillance, bans on political protests). Furthermore, a decision by Justice Secretary Ken Clark to reduce the use of short prison sentences created a strong cross party consensus among members from Labour, the Liberal Democrats and liberal elements among the Conservatives.

What compromises did both parties make?

Here we should consider coalition policies where there is disagreement between the parties but where compromises have been made. The main examples are the following:

■ The Trident programme, and final decisions regarding its scale, has been put 'on hold' and no expenditure will be committed for some years to come.

■ Making income tax more favourable for married couples is proposed in the coalition agreement, but opposed by Liberal Democrats. Liberal Democrat MPs will be allowed to abstain (i.e. not vote at all) if this is brought to a vote in the House of Commons.

■ The compromise on nuclear energy is that Liberal Democrats will be able to vote against further expansion of the programme (it is expected that Labour will support a future nuclear energy programme).

■ Conservatives are very much opposed to Britain adopting the euro or giving over any more sovereignty to the European Union. As a compromise, it is promised that nothing will change until after the next election and, thereafter, a change will be subject to a referendum.

■ The proposal to introduce electoral reform is a compromise. Conservatives have allowed a referendum on a change to the Alternative Vote system, but most members of the party will oppose it. The Liberal Democrats will support the change, but, ultimately, the electorate will decide.

■ It is likely that the arrangements for the protection of human rights in the UK will be strengthened, something which both parties support, but there will be no surrendering of parliamentary sovereignty to a new Bill of Rights, something the Liberal Democrats would like to see.

■ Cameron's idea of the 'Big Society' will probably be tolerated by Liberal Democrats, though they fear it may become a substitute for effective state action to improve local services and environments.

This is not an exhaustive list and, if the coalition is to survive, more compromises will have to be made. However, it does indicate that the coalition agreement was an example of how much two parties, both of which wish to retain power until at least 2015, are willing to compromise.

A 'blueprint' for the future?

Asking this question effectively means considering whether there are any 'ideological' aspects to this agreement. In other words, are there significant elements of genuine consensus to be found in the agreement? Both fundamental consensus and ideological conflicts which remain should be considered.

Fundamental consensus
- Both parties seem determined to protect civil liberties and reduce the extent to which the state controls the actions of individuals.
- There is agreement that local communities should have more autonomy and that most services should enjoy decentralised management.
- The two parties accept the need to restore responsible public financing as quickly as is feasible and to maintain a responsible approach to government borrowing.
- There is a good deal of consensus over the need to speed up the development of renewable energy sources and to introduce more stringent targets on emissions control. This is despite the fact that the two parties disagree over nuclear energy.
- The two parties agree (along with the Labour Party) on the need to protect and expand, as far as possible within the difficult economic climate, front line services in health and education.
- The parties agree on the need to protect the most 'vulnerable' in British society, mainly those on low wages, the disabled and the elderly. There do, however, remain disagreements over how this is to be achieved and the extent to which the richer elements in society should be made to pay for this protection.
- Both parties acknowledge the need for constitutional reform, notably reform of both Houses of Parliament, freedom of information and human rights, though they do not agree over the nature of electoral reform.

Fundamental divisions
Here we must consider the lack of consensus and therefore evidence that the coalition and its agreement do *not* represent a 'blueprint for the future', but will be only a temporary arrangement.

- Liberal Democrats and Conservatives do not agree about Britain's future defence requirements. The conflict centres on nuclear weapons and is affected greatly by differences over foreign policy. While Conservatives still see Britain as a 'major player' in world affairs and a staunch ally of the USA, Liberal Democrats accept that Britain's role should be both more limited and more 'ethical' or critical of US policy.
- Britain's relationship with the European Union can cause a major rift between the two coalition partners. While the Liberal Democrats wish to see the UK eventually adopting the euro and taking a more integrated role

in Europe, the Conservatives have ruled out any possibility that the UK will join the single currency and wish to see a 'looser' political union in Europe.

- The Liberal Democrats have radical proposals for constitutional reform in several areas — the electoral system, a codified constitution, the second chamber, human rights and the future of devolution. Conservatives under Cameron support some degree of reform but their proposals are very limited and they do not wish to support any *fundamental* change.

- The Liberal Democrats see themselves as the main home for those who support radical measures to improve social justice and more equality in Britain. Again, Cameron has gone some way to bring the Conservatives closer to liberalism, but the Conservative Party will not support state action to create significantly more economic equality in Britain.

- Both parties claim to be 'business friendly' but this hides a basic distinction. Conservatives see business, large, medium and small, as essential to the economic health of Britain. Liberal Democrats agree, but warn that those who run businesses must show a more responsible attitude towards consumers, employees and the national interest.

Summary

- There is a high level of agreement within the coalition arrangements.
- A number of key compromises have been achieved.
- The consensus between the two parties is largely on a temporary basis, not designed to last beyond 2015.
- There remain a number of fundamental ideological distinctions between the Conservative and Liberal Democrat parties.

Exam focus

To consolidate your knowledge of this chapter, answer the following questions:

1 To what extent is there consensus or adversary politics in Britain following the formation of the coalition government?
2 To what extent have Conservatives compromised their beliefs for the sake of the agreement?
3 To what extent have Liberal Democrats compromised their beliefs for the sake of the agreement?
4 Do modern Conservatives and Liberal Democrats share any common ideological beliefs?

Chapter 5

The coalition and constitutional reform: a new departure?

Exam success

The up-to-date facts, examples and arguments in this chapter will help you to produce good-quality answers in your AS unit tests in the following areas of the specifications:

Edexcel	AQA	OCR
Unit 1	**Unit 1**	**Unit F851**
Elections	Electoral systems	Electoral systems and referenda
Unit 2	**Unit 2**	**Unit F852**
The Constitution	The British Constitution	The Constitution
Parliament	Parliament	The legislature

Context

2010 marked the end of the New Labour experiment. A party that had entered government in 1997 offering an extensive programme of constitutional reform, departed having achieved little of worth in the field since the end of its first term in office in 2001 (see Table 5.2).

While British Conservatism has generally been associated with pragmatism and the desire to maintain cherished traditions, the Conservative–Lib Dem coalition that emerged in the wake of the 2010 general election offered a raft of constitutional proposals every bit as radical as those advanced by New Labour some 13 years before. However, the extent to which such proposals represent a 'new departure' or simply 'more of the same' is open to question.

This chapter considers the coalition government's constitutional reform proposals against the backdrop of what went before under New Labour (1997–2010). In doing so, it answers the following questions:

- What constitutional reforms did the Conservative–Lib Dem coalition offer in the agreement published in May 2010?
- Are any of these proposals likely to find their way into law?
- Is what is proposed really a 'new departure' or simply 'more of the same'?

What constitutional reforms did the coalition offer in the May 2010 agreement?

The coalition agreement concluded between the Conservatives and the Lib Dems in the wake of the inconclusive 2010 general election offered the prospect of significant constitutional reform in a number of different areas (see Table 5.1).

Table 5.1 The coalition agreement on constitutional reform

Parliamentary reform
- A move to 5-year fixed-term parliaments and roughly equal electoral districts
- Recall of MPs where 10% of constituents call for a ballot
- State funding for all-party 'primary elections' in seats that have not changed hands for some time
- A commitment to implement the proposals of the Wright Committee in full
- A new upper chamber, to be wholly or mainly elected under a PR system

Electoral reform
- A Referendum Bill to authorise a public vote on the adoption of the AV system for use in elections to the Westminster Parliament

Democracy and participation
- Measures gaining the support of a petition of 100,000 voters to become eligible for debate in parliament
- The petition carrying the largest number of signatures to be tabled as a bill
- A new 'public reading stage' for bills, allowing members of the general public to comment on bills online
- Residents given the power to initiate local referendums on any local issue
- Voters to be given the power to veto excessive Council Tax rises

Devolution
- Implement the recommendations of the Calman Commission in Scotland
- Hold a referendum on further devolution in Wales
- Review the basis of devolution funding
- A commission to investigate the West Lothian Question

Parliamentary reform

Commons reform

The Reform of the House of Commons Committee — commonly known as the 'Wright Committee' after Dr Tony Wright MP, its chair — published its recommendations for reform of the Commons in November 2009. Though some had feared that the proposals might be lost in the fallout from the 2010 general election, the coalition agreement included a commitment to implement the Committee's recommendations in full — if not all entirely at once. The Committee's main recommendations are set out in Box 5.1.

The Wright Committee's proposals

- To reduce the number and size of Departmental Select Committees
- To require the election of committee chairs by the House of Commons under a secret ballot
- That the remaining members of each committee should be elected by secret ballot within party groups
- To reduce the influence of party whips within such committees
- To give the House direct control of the timetabling of backbench business
- To create a Petitions Committee in order to allow for greater use of e-petitions, with the possibility that parliament might be required to discuss issues achieving a certain level of public support

Lords reform

In the area of Lords reform, the coalition was, in effect, doing little more than underlining its support for that which had been agreed at the end of the cross-party consultation conducted under the previous Labour administration.

Electoral reform

The willingness of David Cameron and his negotiating team to guarantee a referendum on the introduction of the Alternative Vote system (see Box 5.2) in elections to the Westminster parliament was one of the more surprising things to come out of the coalition negotiations. Here was the leader of a party that had traditionally opposed electoral reform, offering the guarantee of a referendum on a system that would almost certainly result in the Conservatives losing seats at the next general election. More amazing still was the fact that the Lib Dems — who had long campaigned for the introduction of proportional representation — were prepared to accept the offer of a system that was in many respects no better than the FPTP (simple plurality) system they sought to replace.

The decision to combine electoral reform with the equalisation of the parliamentary constituencies, a reduction in the number of MPs from 650 to 600, and the introduction of 5-year fixed-term parliaments, will have sweetened the pill for some critics of this proposal. However, the choice of AV is surprising nonetheless. Some Lib Dems might perhaps see this system as a stepping stone on the way to something far better, but adopting it would paradoxically serve only to make the 'Holy Grail' of proportional representation more distant still.

Is AV really that much better than the FPTP system?
Yes, it is

- AV allows for greater voter choice. This is because it is a preferential system, i.e. voters are able to indicate where they would like their vote to go in the event that their preferred candidate is eliminated.

Box 5.2 Alternative Vote (AV)

- AV is a majoritarian system.
- It retains the single member constituencies that exist under FPTP but requires the winning candidate in each constituency to gain 50%+ of the votes cast.
- Instead of putting a cross in a single box, voters have the opportunity to rank candidates in order of preference (1, 2, 3 etc.).
- Any candidate achieving 50%+ of first preference votes is duly elected.
- If no candidate wins on first preferences, the bottom-placed candidate is eliminated and their votes are transferred to other candidates on the basis of the preferences indicated on each ballot paper.
- This process continues until a candidate crosses the 50%+ winning line.

- Parties such as the Lib Dems — which have traditionally fared badly under FPTP because they are often placed second in constituencies — would almost certainly win more seats.
- The AV system will mean that every MP will be able to claim the support of at least half of their constituents, and that a government securing an overall majority in the Commons should always be able to claim the backing of at least half of those who voted (thus enhancing their mandate).

No, it is not
- AV is not a proportional system and can result in an even less proportional outcome than FPTP. For example, it is estimated that Labour would have won 17 more seats and increased their Commons majority from 178 to 213 at the 1997 general election, had AV been used in place of FPTP.
- AV does not give different weightings to first preferences and subsequent preferences once a candidate has failed to win on first preferences alone. This means that a candidate can win the most first preferences yet end up losing the contest.
- AV is unlikely to make any significant difference to the socioeconomic profile of MPs, whereas many proportional systems would be likely to result in the election of more women and candidates from ethnic minorities.

Democracy and participation

Ahead of the 2010 general election, all three major parties made a commitment to encourage greater public participation in politics. While the widening access to broadband internet made it inevitable that many of the new proposals centred on the development of e-democracy (see Box 5.3), it was significant that all three parties also favoured the introduction of recalls — a form of publicly initiated referendum by which an elected official can be removed from office before the end of his or her elected term.

The coalition agreement took on many of these new proposals, while at the same time innovating in other areas. Most remarkable, perhaps, was the suggestion that voters would be given the power of 'initiative' at local level, i.e. that ordinary citizens would be able to initiate changes to local laws and ordinances by petition, confirmed by local referendum. Though such initiatives are widely used in many US states, their operation is not entirely unproblematic.

Should initiatives be used in the UK?

Yes, they should

- Initiatives provide an additional avenue for political participation.
- They allow ordinary citizens to initiate a legislative change rather than having to convince the government of the merit of their cause.
- Initiatives allow citizens to unite and legislate 'over the heads' of a government that is ignoring the will of the popular majority.
- Citizens are able to call public votes on moral issues and other questions that would rarely be put to a public vote by the government of the day.

No, they should not

- Initiatives undermine representative democracy by allowing voters to 'second-guess' the representatives they have elected to legislate on their behalf.
- Initiatives pander to the 'lowest common denominator'. Where such devices are used widely, the questions drafted by citizens often appear to offer overly simplistic solutions or focus on moral issues that provoke an 'emotional' as opposed to a 'rational' response.
- The initiative process can result in a tyranny of the majority. Elected governments sometimes need to be able to go against the popular will in protecting citizens' long-term interests.
- The initiative process undermines the notion of joined-up government because people are only invited to vote on a single issue as opposed to a coherent programme of measures.

Devolution

Devolution is generally seen as one of the success stories of New Labour's constitutional reform programme. It is not surprising, therefore, that the coalition's proposals in this area of policy are more easily seen as evidence of 'continuity' than of 'a new departure'. The promise to implement the main recommendations of the Calman Commission (see *UK Government and Politics Annual Survey 2010*, Chapter 8) was hardly ground-breaking and the offer of a referendum on the further devolution of powers to Wales had

been widely trailed ahead of the 2010 general election. The one issue that could be said to represent a genuine departure was the explicit commitment to 'investigate' the West Lothian Question — something that had been largely overlooked by the outgoing Labour government, despite the token reduction in the number of Scottish constituencies sending MPs to the Westminster parliament from 72 to 59 ahead of the 2005 general election.

Will any of these proposals find their way into law?

Though the scope and scale of the changes proposed in 2010 was impressive, doubts remain over just how much of the coalition's constitutional reform agenda can be fully realised over the course of a single term in office. The obvious lesson that can be learned from New Labour's 13 years in power is that if significant changes are to be made, they will most likely be made early on, while the government has the energy necessary to overcome the opposition that many of these measures will face, from the Labour opposition, from the governing parties' own backbenches and from the Lords. It is also worth remembering that despite enjoying majorities of 178 (following the 1997 general election), 166 (2001) and 65 (2005), the Labour Party still failed to realise its vision in many areas of constitutional reform (see Table 5.2). The coalition, enjoying only a fairly modest Commons majority, will be seeking to deliver policies on which it will struggle even to maintain discipline within its own ranks.

Table 5.2 New Labour's record on constitutional reform

1997 manifesto pledge on...	
Lords reform	**Success or failure?**
▪ To 'remove the right of hereditary peers to sit and vote' in the Lords ▪ To reform the Lords to make it more 'democratic and representative'	▪ The House of Lords Act (1998) removed the rights of all but 92 hereditary peers to sit and vote in the Lords ▪ Lords reform stalled thereafter in the absence of a clear consensus
Commons reform	**Success or failure?**
▪ To establish an investigation into House procedures ▪ To make Prime Minister's Questions 'more effective' ▪ To regulate party funding ▪ To offer a referendum on electoral reform once an independent commission has made its recommendations	▪ The Wright Committee published its recommendations in November 2009 ▪ Though PMQs became a single 30-minute slot (as opposed to two 15-minute slots), its reputation was not greatly enhanced as a result ▪ The PPERA (2000) failed to prevent further scandals regarding party funding; the issue rumbled on ▪ Labour established the Jenkins' Commission but ignored the Commission's central recommendation: that AV+ should be used in place of FPTP at UK general elections

1997 manifesto pledge on…	
Open government	**Success or failure?**
■ To introduce a 'Freedom of Information Act'	■ The Freedom of Information Act (2000) did not come into force until 2005 ■ Critics argued that it fell short of what had been hoped for
Devolution	**Success or failure?**
■ To hold Scottish and Welsh devolution referendums by the autumn of 1997 (with no threshold) ■ To offer the Scots a parliament with both primary legislative powers and 'tax varying powers' ■ To offer the Welsh an assembly with 'secondary legislative powers'	■ Labour delivered on its central pledges ■ Critics argued that the changes failed to address the West Lothian Question ■ Though devolution was widely seen as a success, the ultimate 'end-point' of the devolution programme remained unclear
Good local government	**Success or failure?**
■ To give greater power to local councils ■ To provide for a proportion of councillors to be 'elected annually' to promote 'greater accountability' ■ To introduce elected mayors with 'executive powers' in some cities ■ To establish a new 'strategic authority' and mayor for London ■ To hold referendums, 'region by region', on the creation of directly elected regional governments	■ The first two proposals were not realised ■ Some areas did adopt the proposals for directly elected mayors (e.g. Hartlepool) ■ The Greater London Authority was established, comprising the Mayor of London and the Greater London Assembly ■ Voters in a referendum held in the northeast rejected the offer of a regional assembly; plans for subsequent referendums in other regions were scrapped
Real rights for citizens	**Success or failure?**
■ To incorporate the European Convention on Human Rights (ECHR) into UK law as a 'floor', not a 'ceiling', for the rights of UK citizens ■ To establish legally enforceable rights for the disabled	■ The Human Rights Act (1998) came into force in October 2000 ■ The Labour government was accused of undermining this legislation in the wake of the terrorist attacks on 9/11 and 7/7 ■ Labour established the Disability Rights Commission in 1999; the body was subsumed into the Equality Commission in the wake of the Equality Act (2006)
Northern Ireland	**Success or failure?**
■ To build on the Anglo-Irish Agreement, the Downing Street Declaration and the Framework Document to move towards the establishment of a devolved legislative body	■ Significant powers were devolved to Northern Ireland, but direct rule was restored between 2002 and 2007 in the wake of renewed paramilitary violence ■ By 2010, devolved powers had been restored and extended into areas such as policing

Is what is proposed really a 'new departure'?

It is clear that many of the constitutional changes proposed by the coalition government build on what has gone before, as opposed to being truly innovative. Though the promise of fixed-term parliaments and some of the proposals designed to enhance direct participation in policy making at local and national levels are more ground-breaking, even they might be seen as drawing on Gordon Brown's earlier attempts to subject prerogative powers to Commons scrutiny and engage with the public through devices such as Citizens' Juries and Citizens' Assemblies.

The most obvious sense in which the recent proposals can be seen as a new departure, therefore, is the way in which a party long associated with pragmatism and maintaining cherished traditions has come to accept the need for radical as opposed to incremental change.

Summary

- The coalition agreement offered the prospect of a 'second wave' of constitutional reform, following on from significant changes made in the late 1990s.
- While it is likely that some of the proposals carried over from the previous government will remain problematic (e.g. Lords Reform) and others may fail to gain the necessary support in the referendums planned (e.g. electoral reform), many of the other proposals (e.g. fixed-term parliaments, experiments in e-democracy) are likely to pass into law.
- While the changes proposed should be seen as a continuation of the process started under New Labour — as opposed to 'a new departure' — the decision to embrace such changes should certainly be seen as a 'new departure' for a Conservative Party traditionally associated with pragmatism in the field of constitutional reform.

Exam focus

To consolidate your knowledge of this chapter, answer the following questions:

1 What were the main proposals for constitutional reform in the May 2010 coalition agreement?
2 Should the electoral system used for elections to the Westminster parliament be changed to a PR system? Give reasons to support your answer.
3 To what extent do you agree with the view that initiatives undermine representative democracy?
4 Are the coalition government's proposals for constitutional reform a new departure or more of the same? Give reasons to support your answer.

Chapter 6

Ed Miliband: what next for Labour?

Exam success

The up-to-date facts, examples and arguments in this chapter will help you to produce good-quality answers in your AS unit tests in the following areas of the specifications:

Edexcel	AQA	OCR
Unit 1	Unit 1	Unit F851
Party policies and ideas	Political parties	Political parties

Context

Labour's 'defeat' at the 2010 general election and the emergence of a viable Conservative–Lib Dem coalition in the days that followed, precipitated Gordon Brown's resignation, both as prime minister and party leader. Thus, in the depths of defeat, the Labour Party was forced into a leadership election, which many in the party had wanted a year or even 2 years earlier, when there was still time to right things ahead of the election. Whereas Gordon Brown had been unchallenged when succeeding Tony Blair as Labour leader in 2007 — in spite of the desperate behind-the-scenes efforts of Charles Clarke and others to come up with a suitable alternative — the 2010 leadership election was to be a proper contest. Crucially, however, this was a contest to choose the leader of the opposition, not to choose a leader who might reasonably expect to become prime minister any time soon. With the coalition committed to a general election in 2015, the best candidate for the job of Labour leader in 2010 would not necessarily be the best person for the job *per se*.

This chapter provides an outline of the Labour leadership contest of 2010 and an assessment of the way in which the Labour Party leader is selected. It also considers what Ed Miliband's victory could mean for the party and will answer the following questions:

- In what direction is Ed Miliband likely to take the Labour Party?
- Is the system by which the Labour Party elects its leaders fair?
- Who were the main leadership contenders in 2010 and why did Ed Miliband win?

In what direction is Ed Miliband likely to take the Labour Party?

Although the Labour leadership contest was somewhat overshadowed by the media circus surrounding the formation of the UK's first coalition government since the 1920s, it was a significant event nonetheless.

- First, because it saw New Labour's 'Class of 1997' hand over to a representative of a new generation of Labour politicians drawn from the ranks of special advisors.
- Second, because it was said to mark the end of the New Labour project.

Ed Miliband's election as leader therefore raises serious questions about the direction in which the party is likely to move over the course of the next few years.

Should we see Miliband as 'Red Ed'?

Yes, we should

- Ed Miliband's victory in the race to succeed Brown resulted in no small part from his ability to secure the endorsement of the larger trade unions.
- As will be discussed later in this chapter, Ed Miliband secured fewer votes than his brother David among both the Parliamentary Labour Party (PLP) and individual Labour Party members.
- Union backing for Ed Miliband appeared to result from both his willingness to attack New Labour's record in government and his acceptance of the need for the party to get 'back to basics'.

No, we should not

- Although the younger Miliband largely succeeded in positioning himself as an 'outsider' in the 2010 leadership contest, he was clearly nothing of the kind.
- Like his brother David and fellow leadership contender Ed Balls, Ed Miliband had worked as a special advisor prior to becoming an MP. Indeed, he was one of those special advisors fast-tracked into the Commons on their way to ministerial positions by being selected as candidates in Labour safe-seats (see *UK Government and Politics Annual Survey 2006*).
- Ed Miliband's record as an MP and a minister is in fact characterised by loyalty and conformity as opposed to rebellion. According to the monitoring website TheyWorkForYou.com, the MP for Doncaster North consistently supported government policy following his election to the Commons in 2005, voting in favour of allowing ministers to intervene in inquests, supporting ID cards, opposing an official investigation into the Iraq War, and backing a stricter asylum system.
- While such positions were required by collective responsibility once Miliband had assumed a cabinet position in 2007, they are hardly consistent with the 'Red Ed' tag.

Crucial to the outcome of the 2010 leadership contest was the degree to which the younger Miliband's lower profile in government allowed him to portray himself as the party outsider, despite the fact that he had been responsible for drafting the party's election manifesto. David Miliband and Ed Balls, in contrast, were more closely associated with the outgoing government and therefore appeared reluctant to undermine Labour's (and, by implication, their own) record in office.

While the more conservative-leaning tabloids were happy to be able to label the victorious Miliband as 'Red Ed', their true motivation for coining the 'tag' was to portray him as an ideological extremist, rather than to encapsulate his approach to politics. As the *Guardian*'s Michael White recognised, 'Red Ed is the Miliband of choice for the coalition and its Fleet Street allies, who will be sharpening their knives on the unions' choice.' Moreover, as Tony Blair remarked in the wake of Miliband's victory, taking the party back towards the left wing would only risk undoing everything that the Labour Party reformists since Neil Kinnock had set out to achieve. The party could simply end up repeating the mistakes made during Michael Foot's brief tenure as leader in the early 1980s (see Box 6.1).

Miliband's first few weeks in post provided few clues as to precisely where he might look to position the party between now and 2015. For example, while he publicly recognised that New Labour had underestimated the scale of the economic crisis (suggesting he wanted to make a clear break with the past), Miliband responded to the news that fire-fighters intended to take industrial action on 5 November by affirming his belief that there was no place for 'irresponsible industrial action' (echoing the New Labour mantra on industrial relations).

The comprehensive 2-year Labour Party policy review launched by Miliband at the end of November 2010 will mean members of the shadow cabinet chairing policy groups that will report back to the party's annual conference in 2011. However, this move was widely seen as an attempt to kick into the long grass the ongoing debate over what positions the party should adopt in opposition.

Box 6.1 The Labour Party in the early 1980s

In the wake of Labour's defeat at the 1979 general election, party left-wingers under the leadership of Michael Foot took control. They argued that the party's decline in the late 1970s and more specifically its defeat in the 1979 election had resulted from a 'drift to the right' under the former leader James Callaghan. The left-wingers believed that Labour needed to re-engage with its base by returning to a more consistently socialist platform. However, far from reinvigorating the base, Foot's leadership in fact contributed to a landslide defeat at the 1983 general election — where Labour's manifesto was dubbed 'the longest suicide note in history' — and an extended period in opposition.

Is Ed Miliband simply a caretaker-leader?

The very real danger in taking on the leadership of a party exhausted after more than a decade in office and foundering in the wake of a general election defeat is that one may never be anything more than leader of the opposition. Such was the fate of William Hague, who succeeded John Major as Conservative leader in 1997 and resigned following the party's defeat at the 2001 general election. We should also remember that Hague's successor, Iain Duncan Smith, was forced to step down in 2003, before he even had the opportunity to lead his party into a general election campaign.

It is therefore likely that at least some of those who supported Ed Miliband did so not because they regarded him as the 'next Labour prime minister' but instead as someone who could lead the party through a period of soul searching and reassessment on the opposition benches. After all, the Labour Party had three leaders between James Callaghan and Tony Blair, just as the Tories had three leaders between John Major and David Cameron.

Is the Labour Party leadership electoral system fair?

The Labour Party elects its leaders using an Electoral College operating under a preferential voting system.

Nomination of candidates
- Only Labour MPs are eligible to stand for election to the post of Labour leader.
- Where the leadership falls vacant (following the resignation or death of the incumbent), prospective candidates must seek the support of 12.5% of the Commons members of the Parliamentary Labour Party. In 2010, this meant that prospective candidates needed to secure the backing of 33 Labour MPs.
- Where there is no vacancy for leader, those seeking to challenge the incumbent must secure the backing of 20% of Labour MPs ahead of the annual party conference.
- Further obstacles are put in place in respect of leadership challenges that occur when the party is in government.

The Electoral College
- The election takes place using an Electoral College divided into three equal voting 'sections' (see Table 6.1).
- Since the 1994 leadership election, all sections have voted on a one-member-one-vote (OMOV) basis.
- Voting operates on a preferential basis, i.e. those casting a ballot are allowed to rank candidates in order of preference, as opposed to simply voting for a single candidate.

Table 6.1 Labour's Electoral College

Section 1	The Commons members of the Parliamentary Labour Party (i.e. Labour MPs) and members of the European PLP (i.e. Labour MEPs)
Section 2	Individual members of the Labour Party
Section 3	Members of affiliated organisations who have indicated their support for the party and are not members of another political party

- Any candidate securing more than 50% of the votes cast is duly elected. Where no candidate secures more than half of the votes, a further 'ballot' takes place. The bottom-ranked candidate is eliminated and their votes are transferred in line with the preferences indicated on the ballot papers.
- This process continues until one candidate secures at least 50% of votes.

Is the system fair?

Yes, the system is fair

- The Electoral College system puts individual party members on an equal footing with MPs/MEPs and members of affiliated organisations. This is a big improvement on the system used between 1922 and 1980, where only members of the Parliamentary Labour Party were permitted to vote.
- The voting for all three sections now operates on an OMOV basis.
- The weighting of the union vote was reduced from 40% to 33.33% in 1993.
- It is right that unions and other affiliated organisations retain a say in electing the party leader as they played a crucial role in founding the Labour Party back in the early 1900s.

No, the system is not fair

- There are far more individual party members than MPs/MEPs, yet these two sections get an equal say under the Electoral College.
- The unions still have a massive input despite the fact that most of the people they represent are not regular members of the Labour Party.
- The nomination rules prevent some candidates who might be popular outside of the Commons PLP from qualifying for the ballot.
- There may be no election at all where only one candidate is nominated (as with Gordon Brown in 2007). This deprives party members and affiliated organisations of any role in the process.
- As in 2010, a candidate can win even though they do not have majority support among either the PLP or individual party members.

Who were the main contenders and why did Ed Miliband win?

By the time the deadline for nominations passed on 9 June 2010, five candidates had secured the 33 nominations required to qualify for the ballot (see Table 6.2). This was the largest field to contest the Labour leadership since 1976.

Although five candidates qualified for the leadership ballot, three of the five stood little realistic chance of winning the race to succeed Gordon Brown:

- Diane Abbott was never seen as a genuine challenger, with even most of her supporters accepting that her candidature was more about ensuring that the field did not consist entirely of white men in their 30s and 40s with limited experience of life beyond Westminster.
- Andy Burnham had some experience but lacked the public profile and persona.

Table 6.2 2010 Labour leadership contenders

Candidate	Background
Diane Abbott (33 nominations)	■ Britain's first black woman MP ■ Stood because she felt that that the other candidates were too similar, in terms of both their career paths and their political outlook ■ A left-winger and serial backbench rebel in Commons votes between 1997 and 2010 ■ The only candidate who had opposed the Iraq war ■ A regular on BBC One's *This Week* show ■ No frontbench experience
Ed Balls (33 nominations)	■ Former special advisor to Gordon Brown at the Treasury ■ An MP since 2005 ■ Secretary for Schools and Children under Brown from 2007 ■ Seen as a Brownite
Andy Burnham (33 nominations)	■ A former parliamentary researcher ■ An MP since 2001 ■ Health Secretary under Brown; previously Culture Secretary and Chief Secretary to the Treasury ■ Seen as a Blairite
David Miliband (81 nominations)	■ Former special advisor to Tony Blair and head of the Policy Unit ■ An MP since 2001 ■ Long regarded as a leadership contender ■ Foreign Secretary under Brown ■ Seen as a Blairite
Ed Miliband (63 nominations)	■ Special advisor to Gordon Brown ■ An MP since 2005 ■ Entered cabinet under Brown as the Minister for the Cabinet Office; later served as Energy and Climate Change Secretary ■ Authored Labour's 2010 general election manifesto

Source: 'Labour leadership contest: runners and riders', BBC news online.

■ Ed Balls was seen as overly combative and was too closely associated with the Brown camp.

The result was a 'two-horse race' between David Miliband — the man who many had assumed would one day lead the party — and his younger brother, Ed. Although David Miliband was regarded as the favourite at the outset, his brother had two significant advantages in the race to succeed Brown:

■ First, Ed Miliband was not (rightly or wrongly) as closely associated with New Labour's period in office — having only entered parliament in 2005 and subsequently taken on a number of lower-profile ministerial portfolios.

- Second, David Miliband's failure to mount a challenge to Brown either in 2007 (when Blair stood down) or in the summer of 2008 (when talk of a Blairite leadership coup was rife) suggested indecision and lack of conviction on the part of the older Miliband.

Crucially, Ed Miliband's ability to distance himself from the outgoing New Labour administration and attract the endorsement of larger unions such as the GMB meant that he was able to secure victory in the fourth and final ballot even though he failed to win the support of a majority of the PLP or individual party members in any of the ballots and trailed his older brother overall in the first three rounds (see Table 6.3).

Table 6.3 Results of the 2010 Labour leadership contest (% share of the vote)

First ballot				
Candidate	MPs/MEPs	Members	Affiliates	Total
Diane Abbott	**0.88**	**2.45**	**4.09**	**7.42 (eliminated)**
Ed Balls	5.01	3.37	3.41	11.79
Andy Burnham	3.01	2.85	2.83	8.68
David Miliband	13.91	14.69	9.18	37.78
Ed Miliband	10.53	9.98	13.82	34.33
Total	33.33	33.33	33.33	100.00

Second ballot				
Candidate	MPs/MEPs	Members	Affiliates	Total
Ed Balls	5.18	3.83	4.22	13.23
Andy Burnham	**3.03**	**3.30**	**4.08**	**10.41 (eliminated)**
David Miliband	14.02	15.08	9.80	38.89
Ed Miliband	11.11	11.13	15.23	37.47

Third ballot				
Candidate	MPs/MEPs	Members	Affiliates	Total
Ed Balls	**5.43**	**4.82**	**5.77**	**16.02 (eliminated)**
David Miliband	15.78	16.08	10.86	42.72
Ed Miliband	12.12	12.43	16.71	41.26

Fourth ballot				
Candidate	MPs/MEPs	Members	Affiliates	Total
David Miliband	17.81	18.14	13.40	49.35
Ed Miliband	**15.52**	**15.20**	**19.93**	**50.65 (elected)**

Source: Labour Party website (www2.labour.org.uk/votes-by-round).

Summary

- Ed Miliband's victory in the 2010 Labour leadership contest resulted from his ability to campaign as a left-leaning 'party outsider', thereby attracting the endorsement of many powerful trade unions such as the GMB.
- David Miliband lost the contest despite winning the majority of votes cast by both the Parliamentary Labour Party and individual members in each of the four ballots, bringing the democratic credentials of Labour's Electoral College into question.
- Despite the 'Red Ed' label, the younger Miliband's record in parliament and in cabinet offers little to suggest that he will lead the Labour Party significantly to the left. Some argue that a re-adoption of the more orthodox socialist positions advocated by some trade unions would return the party to the electoral wilderness it inhabited under the leadership of Michael Foot in the early 1980s.

Exam focus

To consolidate your knowledge of this chapter, answer the following questions:

1 Why did the more conservative-leaning tabloids label Ed Miliband 'Red Ed'?
2 Explain how the Labour Party elects its leader.
3 To what extent do you agree with the view that this is a fair way to elect a party leader?
4 Why did Ed Miliband win the leadership contest?

Chapter 7

New Labour 1997–2010: success or failure?

Exam success

The up-to-date facts, examples and arguments in this chapter will help you to produce good-quality answers in your AS unit tests in the following areas of the specifications:

Edexcel	AQA	OCR
Unit 1	**Unit 1**	**Unit F851**
Party policies and ideas	Political parties	Political parties

Context

The Labour Party was removed from power following defeat in the general election of 2010. The 'New Labour project', as it is sometimes known, thus came to an end. New Labour can be traced back to the early 1990s when the then leader, Neil Kinnock, began the long process of transforming the party from its democratic socialist roots towards a new identity as a more moderate social democratic movement. So great was the ultimate change that the party came to be known as 'New Labour'. John Smith, the leader between 1992 and 1994, gathered around him a young team of ambitious politicians, all of whom shared the belief that Labour had to change if it were ever to regain power. In other words, New Labour had to accept that there was a 'post-Thatcher consensus' in Britain which meant that there was widespread support for free-market capitalism, low taxation and a reduced role for the state. Among this group were Tony Blair, who became leader following Smith's sudden death in 1992, Gordon Brown, Peter Mandelson, Robin Cook and Jack Straw. New Labour swept to power in 1997 on a wave of hope and enthusiasm, led by the Blair group, and remained in power for the next 13 years.

This chapter considers the extent to which Labour governments between 1997 and 2010 were successful in meeting their objectives. In doing so, it answers the following questions:

- What were New Labour's key objectives in 1997?
- In which policy areas was New Labour successful?
- In which policy areas did New Labour fail?
- In which areas was New Labour's performance mixed?
- How successful was New Labour's record in office?

What were New Labour's main objectives in 1997?

- To reduce the level of poverty in the UK, notably child poverty.
- To reduce economic and social inequality.
- To improve social mobility (the ability of individuals to improve their position in society from one generation to the next).
- To create greater equality of opportunity.
- To end the tendency of the economy to move from periods of healthy growth to periods of slump and then back again to growth. This was described by Gordon Brown as 'an end to boom and bust'.
- To make significant improvements in welfare provision, notably health and education.
- To reform the social security system to make work more rewarding and worthwhile and to eliminate the poverty trap which tended to make people reliant on benefits rather than self-reliant.
- To improve the state of democracy in the UK, including better protection of individual rights and freedoms.
- To reduce the incidence of crime and the fear of crime.
- To pursue a more 'ethical' foreign policy while, at the same time, protecting vital British interests.
- To make greater progress towards reducing emissions which contribute to climate change.

How well did Labour perform?

Poverty reduction

The reduction of poverty, especially child poverty, was a key objective of Tony Blair and Gordon Brown. The overall picture is mixed and relatively unimpressive, though not without some success.

If we look at households whose income is less than 60% of the average household income (the most common method), the proportion in poverty *fell* between 1997 and 2009 from 25.3% to 22.3% (see the Poverty Site, www.poverty.org.uk). However, if we look at households at less than 40% of average income, the proportion *rose* in the same period from 8.8% to 9.8%. Thus, poverty fell in general, but more people became *very* poor.

The position for children is a little better. In pure numbers, the number of children living in households earning less than 60% of the national average fell from 3.5 million to 2.8 million. So there are about 700,000 fewer children living in poverty than when Labour took office in 1997. This is encouraging but well behind Brown and Blair's own targets.

Author's verdict: 5/10. There has been some progress, but it is relatively modest, well below Labour's own aspirations, and poverty persists despite the introduction of many policies designed to reduce it.

Social mobility, inequality and equality of opportunity

The picture on social mobility looks disappointing, especially as this a flagship policy objective for Labour. The Social Mobility Commission, set up by the Liberal Democrats, reported early in 2009 and it concluded that Britain's record was poor. In particular, the report pointed out that the huge expansion in higher-education opportunity under Labour had largely benefited the middle classes rather than the children of poorer families. The Commission's chairman commented: 'education has not become the great leveller that many people believed it would be'. The report added that Britain remained 'a society of persistent inequality'.

A Trades Union Congress report (we would expect the trade union movement to be more sympathetic to Labour) in August 2010 reached similar conclusions to that of the Liberal Democrats. In particular, it noted that Britain's performance on improving social mobility lagged behind most of the rest of Europe (though it was ahead of the USA). There is, however, a word of caution needed here. Social mobility statistics inevitably relate to *past generations* and are therefore always out of date in a sense. This means that Britain's poor performance in the 1990s and 2000s is as much caused by past policies as by current ones.

Inequality and equality of opportunity are closely related to social mobility. Labour's main attack on inequality centred on the introduction of the national minimum wage in 1997 and the introduction of tax credits to help working families, families with children and pensioners. Equality of opportunity was to be tackled largely by improving education (schools and higher education) as well as removing barriers to opportunity for women, ethnic minorities and the disabled.

Economic inequality between households can be measured in a number of ways, but normally the Gini coefficient is used. It is not important here to explain how this is calculated, save to say that the higher the coefficient figure, the greater the inequality that exists. In the UK, the Gini coefficient rose from 37 in 1996–97 to 40 in 2008–09. This change speaks for itself. Another way of looking at this rise in inequality is to examine the position of the richest tenth and the poorest tenth of the population. Between 1999 and 2009, the incomes of the top tenth rose by an average of 37% while those of the bottom tenth fell by 12% (see the Poverty Site, www.poverty.org.uk). In other words, whatever measure is used, inequality *grew* in the UK under Labour (though it should be pointed out that it also grew markedly in the 1980s under the Conservatives).

Author's verdict: 4/10. Labour can be especially criticised as this area of social policy is at the very core of its political philosophy.

Economic growth and stability

We can divide this judgement into two periods, 1997–2007 and 2007–10. In the first period, Britain enjoyed an unprecedented run of consistent economic

growth. For 10 years, national income grew steadily by between 2 and 4% per annum. These growth rates were faster than in Germany, France and Japan and not far behind the USA. At the same time during this period, inflation remained low, as did interest rates. Unemployment was low and falling. House prices rose consistently, creating a sense of economic well-being and boosting consumer spending.

The second period began with the credit crunch of 2007 and the recession which followed it. This was marked by a fall in national income for the first time since the early 1990s. Unemployment began to rise, as did inflation, though interest rates fell (reduced by the Bank of England to try to encourage borrowing and growth). House prices did not fall as had been feared. Above all, however, the government was forced to run up a huge deficit as it had to borrow heavily to pump funds into the failing banking system and to reduce some taxes to stimulate spending.

We can say, therefore, that Gordon Brown and Tony Blair did indeed bring an end to 'boom and bust' for 10 years. They also created a remarkable period of economic stability and growth in the UK. Critics, however, will point out that this was achieved at the expense of financial responsibility. They argue that Gordon Brown ignored the growing crisis in the banking system and that much of the growth had been financed through reckless borrowing by consumers and irresponsible lending by banks.

Author's verdict: 6/10. The credit crunch and economic recession were world problems, largely originating in the USA. The growth between 1997 and 2007 did give the opportunity for government to spend heavily on health, education and transport infrastructure. In other words, the funds generated by growth were not wasted. However, Gordon Brown should have known that the growth was based on shaky foundations.

Health and education

Two important notes of reservation need to be made before considering New Labour's record on health and education provision. The first is that the party set itself stiff targets for improvement and largely failed to achieve those targets. Second, Labour governments increased spending on both by considerable amounts. Between 1998 and 2007, health spending rose by 89%. Education spending, measured as a percentage of total national income, rose from 4.5% to 5.5% in the period 1997–2007. The question needs to be asked, therefore, whether New Labour achieved value for the taxpayers' money.

On the other hand, there were considerable improvements in education and health provision. In 1996–2007, satisfactory literacy levels rose from 78% to 82% at Key Stage 1, from 57% to 80% at Key Stage 2 and from 61% to 74% at Key Stage 3. Meanwhile, the proportion of students achieving five GCSEs at A–C grade rose from 43% to 62%. Places available on degree courses also rose markedly under New Labour. There are many ways of measuring health performance but some key indicators include these: in 1999, nearly 500,000 patients had to wait more than 13 weeks for a first appointment with a consultant. This number had fallen to virtually zero by 2009. Deaths from heart disease fell by 35.4% in 1999–2007, from stroke by 31.4% and from cancer by 13.5%. Nevertheless, the performance on cancer treatment remains modest and is falling below levels enjoyed in the rest of Europe.

Thus, we can see considerable progress in the two areas of health and education, but this has been achieved at a very high cost to the taxpayer.

Author verdict: 6/10. A good deal of improvement was achieved, but below the government's own target and at high cost, and health performance remains below most European levels.

Social security

The introduction of schemes such as 'welfare to work' and tax credits for poor working families, pensioners and single parents was part of a major reform of social security. However, as can be seen in the section above on inequality and poverty reduction, these schemes did not translate as significant progress in social reform. Poverty remains a persistent problem, as does long-term unemployment. There remain many individuals and families who are better off relying on social security than working for a living. In addition, the benefits system has become so complex that it is extremely expensive to run and results in many people falling through the benefits net.

One area has, however, improved. Pensioners are in general much better off than they were in 1997. A range of measures, such as winter fuel payments, free public transport and free TV licences for the over-75s, has helped, but the fact that the state old age pension has steadily risen by above the rate of inflation has done most to improve the lives of the elderly. The Office for National Statistics reported that pensioner poverty (those living on less than 60% of the national average income) fell between 1998 and 2008 by one third, from 2.9 million to 2 million.

Author's verdict: 5/10. Labour failed to reform social security successfully. However, some credit must be given for reductions in poverty among children and pensioners.

Constitutional and democratic reform

From 1997 onwards, Labour governments instigated a major programme of constitutional reform. The crowning glory was, probably, the devolution of power to Scotland, Wales and Northern Ireland. This has proved hugely popular in the British national regions and has broadened the scope of democracy by decentralising power significantly. The Human Rights Act (HRA) has proved to be a successful initiative. Citizens now have a stronger

means by which they can protect their rights and freedoms. The same can be said of the passage of the Freedom of Information Act (FOI). Governments have felt more uncomfortable in having to deal with the HRA and the FOI, but citizens have many reasons to feel safer from arbitrary government as a result. The introduction of the Supreme Court, together with other reforms of the legal system, also went a good way to increasing the independence of the judiciary, a key step towards stronger controls over the abuse of power.

However, these three major developments have to be balanced against less impressive progress. Labour failed to introduce electoral reform for general elections (a 1997 election promise) and its reform of the House of Lords — removing all but 92 hereditary peers — was seen as a weak compromise when there were widespread demands for an elected second chamber. Its programme for the widespread introduction of English regional devolution and elected city mayors (with the notable exception of the London mayor) proved to be unpopular and therefore faltered badly.

Thus, the British political system was significantly reformed by Labour after 1997, having been greatly democratised, decentralised and modernised. But, as with several other policy areas, the reforms fell short of the party's own ambitions.

Author's verdict: 7/10. Constitutional reform is notoriously difficult to implement. Labour did, nevertheless, achieve a great deal and most of the changes have proved to be successful. In the end, however, it remained a 'work in progress'.

Crime reduction

This is perhaps Labour's most notable achievement. Since 1997, crime rates have fallen dramatically, despite some disputes about the accuracy of their measurement. In Labour's first 10 years in office, overall crime levels fell by 35%. In Labour's last year in office, the independent British Crime Survey (BCS) reported a fall of 8% in overall crime. By the time it left office, Labour could claim to have virtually halved the crime rate. The most notable successes have been with burglaries and vehicle crime. Violent crime has fallen less impressively and murder rates have remained broadly flat. The incidence of sexual offences continues to rise (though this may be due to the growing tendency for such crimes to be reported — in the past, they may have remained hidden). Even anti-social behaviour (vandalism, public disorder, drunkenness etc.) was reported by the BCS to have fallen in 2009, despite newspaper reports of a growing problem.

There is a word of caution to be struck here. The prison population had grown to record levels by 2010, at over 82,000. This is the result of more and longer prison sentences being imposed by the courts. Clearly, if more offenders are being held for longer periods in prison, they cannot be committing crimes.

It also has to be noted that Labour governments invested huge quantities of public expenditure on increasing the size of the police force.

Author's verdict: 8/10. Labour's most successful policy area and one for which it does not receive enough credit because of the tabloid press's obsession with reporting individual headline crime but failing to mention the 'big picture'.

Ethical foreign policy

Labour introduced a policy known as 'ethical foreign policy', which was designed to ensure that all foreign initiatives would take account of international law and would be based on respect for the sovereignty of other states and a determination to seek to promote the causes of democracy and human rights. Interventions in the Kosovo war of independence and in Sierra Leone, where a democratic government sought Britain's help against an armed insurrection, seemed to confirm this commitment to international justice. All this was derailed, however, when Tony Blair chose to join the USA and other allies in the Iraq war in 2003. It has since been acknowledged that the war was probably unlawful and the aftermath of the conflict proved to be disastrous for Western policy in the Middle East. Labour governments were also accused of being 'soft' on authoritarian regimes in China and Burma.

So, the ethical foreign policy proved to be a hollow commitment and Britain resorted to its traditional position of supporting American foreign policy uncritically. The war in Afghanistan is a typical example of this.

Author's verdict: 4/10. Labour made a good start, but the Iraq war ruined the government's credibility both at home and abroad.

Environment

The 2008 Climate Change Act was a ground-breaking initiative by the Labour government. The Act, the first of its kind in the world, creates a legally binding commitment for Britain to reduce harmful emissions by 80% by the year 2050. At the time, no other country had made such a commitment. Thus, in terms of its *intentions*, Britain has taken a lead in environmental policy.

The actual record of Labour in terms of climate change and environmental protection, on the other hand, is mixed. On renewable energy production, progress has been slow. The targets set by Labour are that renewable energy sources should account for 10% of total energy by the end of 2010, and 20% by 2020. Both these targets, Labour has admitted, will be missed. The expansion of wind power has been especially disappointing. There have, however, been successes in terms of the reduction in harmful emissions. Under the international Kyoto Agreement, Labour committed the UK to reducing its harmful emissions by 12.5% between 1990 and 2012. In 2008, the government was able to report that emissions had already fallen by 19.4% so Britain was well ahead of its international commitments.

Author's verdict: 6/10. Labour scores well on intentions and world leadership. It has also done well on reducing harmful greenhouse gas emissions (helped by the 2007–09 recession). Its record on renewable energy production has, however, been disappointing.

Summary

The author's overall score for Labour is 51/90. At first sight, this seems to be quite satisfactory — possibly a 'B/C borderline' grade at A-level government and politics. However, it has to be stressed that, on its 'flagship' policies of reducing inequality, reducing poverty and improving social mobility, Labour has been disappointing in relation to its own aspirations. On the other hand, this assessment does not include Northern Ireland. Arguably Labour's greatest achievement of all was to bring peace (with the exception of some remaining unrest) to the province. It must also be emphasised that these verdicts are the opinion only of this author; others may judge New Labour's performance more harshly or more sympathetically.

Exam focus

To consolidate your knowledge of this chapter, answer the following questions:

1 What were New Labour's main policy objectives in 1997?
2 To what extent was New Labour a 'reforming party'?
3 Did New Labour end the era of 'boom and bust'?
4 How successful was New Labour in achieving its main objectives?

Chapter 8

Gordon Brown: a flawed and failed prime minister?

Exam success

The up-to-date facts, examples and arguments in this chapter will help you to produce good-quality answers in your AS unit tests in the following areas of the specifications:

Edexcel	AQA	OCR
Unit 2	Unit 2	Unit F852
The prime minister and cabinet	The core executive	The executive

Context

In August 2010, a poll of academics compiled by Professor Kevin Theakston, from the University of Leeds, found that Gordon Brown was considered the third worst prime minister of the last 65 years, ahead only of Sir Alec Douglas-Home and Sir Anthony Eden, who led Britain into the Suez invasion. How did it all go wrong for Gordon Brown in such a short space of time? Was Gordon Brown a better prime minister than his reputation suggests? This chapter reviews the premiership of Gordon Brown and in doing so answers the following questions:

- Why did Brown and Labour lose the 2010 election?
- What were Gordon Brown's main successes?
- What were his main failures?
- What circumstances weakened his premiership?
- Was Brown a flawed and failed prime minister?

Why did Brown and Labour lose the 2010 general election?

To put the 2010 Labour performance in context, this was the party's worst result since the disastrous 1983 election when Margaret Thatcher won a huge Conservative majority against a hopelessly divided Labour Party. The Labour share of the 2010 votes, at 29%, was its lowest since the Second World War, apart from the 1983 catastrophe. Perhaps more startlingly, the number of Labour votes fell from 13.52 million in 1997 to 8.61 million in 2010. Labour had lost 5 million voters in its 13 years in office. Of course, not all this can be laid at Gordon Brown's door. His predecessor, Tony Blair, was discredited by the experience of the Iraq war in 2003 as well as a decline in his own personal standing. We can, however, identify a number of factors in Labour's defeat which can be directly linked to Gordon Brown.

What were Gordon Brown's main aims in 2007?

- Further improvements in education provision, including higher education
- Reducing inequality in society
- Continuing progress in the eradication of world poverty
- Creating a stronger sense of 'Britishness' among all sections of society
- Restoring public faith in politics
- Giving greater powers to parliament and reducing executive control of parliament
- Improving the performance of the health service, notably that of family doctors
- Building more houses, broadening home ownership and reducing homelessness

How did Brown contribute to Labour's defeat?

- Brown was unable to present a sympathetic public image. He was seen as humourless, dour, out of touch, aloof and, quite simply, dull. Few doubted his intelligence, but this is not enough for the public and the media. In the televised leadership debates which took place during the election campaign, Brown performed poorly, especially compared to Nick Clegg.

- Brown ran a relatively lacklustre election campaign. However, one incident was seen as the point at which all hope for Labour was lost. Having been challenged on immigration policy by Gillian Duffy, a Labour supporter, Brown was overheard referring to her as a bigot when he was not aware his personal microphone had been left on. The subsequent broadcasting of Brown's gaffe provoked widespread condemnation, especially as it was seen as proof that Brown was 'out of touch'.

- The decision to abolish the 10% tax band (the standard rate of tax was reduced from 22% to 20%) from April 2008 for those on low incomes was a disaster for Brown. It meant that poor families would be paying *more* tax than before and so contributing to creating *more* inequality, not less, as Brown had promised.

- It is generally believed that, had Brown called a general election in autumn 2007, shortly after he had succeeded Blair as prime minister, Labour would have won. Brown, however, decided against taking the risk after much delay and indecision. This created a reputation of indecisiveness in Brown, a reputation he could never shake off even when he appeared more decisive in how he dealt with the 'credit crunch' and banking crisis of 2007–08.

- The Iraq war and more particularly its aftermath were firmly blamed on Tony Blair and his government. Brown failed to disassociate himself from policy in Iraq and so shared much of that blame.

- Brown clearly had a persuasive argument in saying that the credit crunch and economic recession which followed were not the responsibility of past Labour governments. He could also claim that most of his time as Chancellor had been marked by growing prosperity. In addition, he could claim to have dealt with the crisis well and to have received much praise from abroad. But Brown was unable to dispel charges that he had been largely responsible for the crisis by failing to control the expansion of credit and by spending irresponsibly.

- Brown had promised that he would 'clean up politics' but his government remained tainted with claims that it was 'all spin and no substance'. He was unable to convince the media that he was tackling 'spin', especially when he brought his former rival Lord Mandleson back into the government. Mandelson had a reputation as the 'king of spin'.

What factors were outside Brown's control?

Election defeat in 2010 was not solely Brown's responsibility. Some of the main problems he faced included:

- Labour — and Brown himself — had been in office for 13 years. The media and the public were simply bored with Labour.
- The relatively new Conservative leader, David Cameron, seemed young, dynamic and more in touch than Brown, even despite his wealthy upbringing.
- The credit crunch and bank crisis were largely an American problem. All developed economies suffered equally from the crisis.
- The political journalist Andrew Rawnsley published a book about Brown in 2010 which suggested he was a bully who had lost the support of much of his party. Whether or not Rawnsley's verdict was justified, Brown's reputation was severely damaged.
- The scandals of 2009, in which many MPs were accused of claiming expenses to which they were not entitled, were partly and irrationally blamed on the government even though they affected all three main parties.

What were Brown's main successes?

The credit crunch

Above all, Brown could claim that he dealt with the credit crunch, which threatened the whole Western banking system in 2007–08, decisively and successfully. Brown ordered immediate guarantees to protect people's savings, invested government funds in several British banks to prevent them failing and led international measures to protect the international financial markets. He was widely praised for his world leadership in Europe and the USA. He also took decisive action to reduce the economic effects of the crisis by persuading the Bank of England to reduce interest rates and to pump more money into the economy. As a result, the financial system did not collapse and the economic recession was relatively mild and short-lived.

World development

Brown further enhanced his international reputation as a champion of developing countries in the reduction of world poverty. He secured funds for increases in Britain's overseas aid budget and led the world in the cancellation of developing-world debt.

Law and order

As can be seen in Chapter 7, on the performance of New Labour, the 3 years of Brown's premiership saw continued falls in the incidence of crime. The increases in the numbers of police and community support officers coincided with falls in both crime and fear of crime in Britain.

Health and education

As described in Chapter 7, Brown devoted increased funds to health and education, which resulted in more improvements in their performance. This was achieved even in uncertain economic times.

What were Brown's main policy failures?

Inequality

It is especially damning that inequality in Britain continued to grow in Britain despite the fact that its reduction was at the heart of Brown's political philosophy. Some reform of the tax system failed to address the fundamental problem of growing inequality.

Poverty

Overall levels of poverty continued to fall during Brown's premiership but the government under Brown missed its targets by some distance. Again, Brown must be criticised severely here as poverty reduction was one of his flagship policies.

Financial regulation

As noted above, blame for the credit crunch and banking crisis cannot all be attributed to Gordon Brown. However, it could be said that, as both Chancellor for 10 years and then prime minister, Brown failed to be aware that the system of financial regulation that he had created was failing to recognise the dangers to the financial system which had been building up for several years.

Political reform

Brown had promised a new style of politics and political reform to restore public confidence in institutions and processes and to enhance democracy. In the event (and, in his defence, he was overwhelmed by the financial crisis), he did little to reform politics. He cannot be blamed for the scandal over MPs' expenses, but he did fail to promote any effective reforms.

What circumstances weakened Brown's premiership?

It is generally acknowledged that Gordon Brown was not a 'dominant' prime minister. The main reasons for this are:

Personal shortcomings

- He was seen as out of touch, humourless, indecisive and, by some, a bully.
- He presented a poor public image and was not an inspiring speaker. He lacked charisma.
- He did not deal well with the media.
- He did not deal well with members of the public.
- He was a poor election campaigner.

Political weaknesses

- He had never faced the electorate as party leader so he lacked legitimacy.
- He had been elected party leader unopposed by Labour in 2007. Again, this suggested that he was not a legitimate leader.
- He inherited a parliamentary majority of over 60, which seems comfortable, but the presence of about 40 persistent dissidents on the Labour backbenches meant he could not dominate parliament.
- Though he never faced a formal leadership challenge, there were constant rumours of plots against him. This suggested he did not command the full support of his own party.
- Labour appeared a divided party, largely on the basis of Blairites and Brownites. This extended into the cabinet.
- A number of key ministerial resignations weakened his leadership. Among them were Caroline Flint (Europe Minister), James Purnell (Work and Pensions) and David Cairns (Scotland Office), all of whom expressed dissatisfaction with Brown's leadership.

Summary

The main lesson to be learned from Brown's term of office is that a prime minister cannot dominate the political system if he loses **political authority**. Gordon Brown had lost virtually all sources of his authority by 2010, namely:

- He lost the full support of his own party. Though he was never challenged formally, he could not rely on widespread support.
- He could not dominate parliament faced, as he was, by a fragile Commons majority and an often obstructive House of Lords.
- He could not rely on the support of his own cabinet.
- He lost public confidence.
- The media turned decisively against him.

So it can be said that Gordon Brown was a flawed prime minister and suffered a number of important failures, culminating in the loss of power for Labour. To say that he *totally* failed, however, would be an exaggeration.

Exam focus

To consolidate your knowledge of this chapter, answer the following questions:

1 In what ways can Gordon Brown be said to have been an unsuccessful prime minister?

2 Why did Gordon Brown lose his political authority?

3 What are the main limitations on the power of the prime minister?

4 Account for Gordon Brown's failure to win the 2010 general election for Labour.

Chapter 9

The UK Supreme Court: a strengthened judiciary?

Exam success

The up-to-date facts, examples and arguments in this chapter will help you to produce good-quality answers in your AS unit tests in the following areas of the specifications:

Edexcel	AQA	OCR
Unit 2	Unit 2	Unit F852
Judges and civil liberties	The British Constitution	The judiciary

Context

1 October 2010 marked the first anniversary of the opening of the new UK Supreme Court at Middlesex Guildhall, Westminster. While the Law Lords serving in the Appellate Committee of the House of Lords had traditionally acted as the highest court of appeal in the UK, the new Supreme Court — established under the terms of the Constitutional Reform Act (2005) — appeared to offer the prospect of an ultimate court of appeal enjoying a greater degree of operational independence and a far higher public profile than that which had gone before. While the second of these expectations has certainly been realised over the course of the Court's first year in operation, it is questionable whether or not the creation of the new Court truly represents a 'strengthening' of the UK judiciary.

This chapter provides an overview of the work of the Court in its inaugural year. It considers the extent to which the judgements handed down by the Court during this period were significantly different from those delivered by the Law Lords previously and it also addresses the question of whether or not this significant change to the structure of the UK judiciary should be seen in terms of a shift in 'power' or simply a shift in 'presentation' and/or 'perception'. In doing so, it answers the following questions:

- What can we learn from the judgements handed down by the Court in its inaugural year?
- Has the UK judiciary been significantly strengthened as a result of the Court's creation?
- Is the existence of the Court likely to have a significant, if less immediately tangible, impact on the independence and authority of the senior judiciary?

What can we learn from the judgements handed down by the Court?

The early cases heard by the new Court (see Box 9.1) hardly represented a significant departure from that which the Law Lords had done hitherto. This lends credence to the view that the creation of a new UK Supreme Court was more a change of 'form' than of 'substance'. The Court's ruling in the November 2010 *R v Chaytor* case, which related to prosecutions over MPs' expenses, for example, was in keeping with the kinds of rulings handed down by the Law Lords in the past. In a similar vein, the Court's ruling in the case of suspected terrorists whose assets had been seized without trial under the new

Box 9.1 Some early cases before the Court (in reverse chronological order)

1 **Attempts by three MPs to use 'parliamentary privilege' as a means of avoiding criminal prosecution over their expenses: *R v Chaytor & Others* (Appellants) [10 November 2010]**

   The Court dismissed the efforts of three Labour MPs to use parliamentary privilege as a means of having their cases heard by the parliamentary authorities alone, rather than in a criminal court. The Court argued that the law was designed to protect free speech and open debate in parliament rather than allowing MPs to evade prosecution for ordinary crimes they were alleged to have committed.

2 **Detention and police questioning without the right to speak to a lawyer in Scotland: *Cadder* (Appellant) v *Her Majesty's Advocate* (Respondent) (Scotland) [26 October 2010]**

   The Court ruled that the refusal of Scottish police officers to allow a suspect to speak to a lawyer prior to questioning was incompatible with the European Convention on Human Rights as incorporated into UK law under the Human Rights Act (1998).

3 **The extent of the Scottish Parliament's legislative powers: *Martin v Her Majesty's Advocate (Scotland); Miller v Her Majesty's Advocate (Scotland)* [3 March 2010]**

   The Court ruled that the Scottish Parliament had acted within its legislative powers in allowing Sheriffs to impose longer prison sentences than those allowed under the Road Traffic Act (1988) when individuals were caught driving while disqualified.

4 **The Treasury's freezing of the assets of suspected terrorists: *HM Treasury v Mohammed Jabar Ahmed & Others; HM Treasury v Mohammed al-Ghabra; R (on the application of Hani El Sayed Sabaei Youssef) v HM Treasury* [27 January 2010]**

   The Court ruled that the UK Treasury had acted *ultra vires* (i.e. beyond the authority granted) when implementing parts of the Terrorism (United Nations Measures) Order 2006 (TO) and the Al-Qaida and Taliban (United Nations Measures) Order 2006 (AQO). These Orders allowed the authorities to freeze the assets of those suspected of terrorist activities without trial — a power that the Court ruled undermined fundamental rights.

anti-terror regime was not so very different in tone or scope from those handed down previously in respect of the indefinite detention of terrorist suspects at Belmarsh under the Anti-terrorism Crime and Security Act (2001) or the use of control orders introduced under the Prevention of Terrorism Act (2005).

In simple terms, therefore, the Court was doing little more than using those powers that had been available to the Law Lords previously when clarifying the legal position in cases where the law itself was unclear, issuing *ultra vires* rulings, making 'declarations of incompatibility' under the Human Rights Act (1998) or adjudicating on disputes arising under EU law.

> **Box 9.2** **Problems that prompted the creation of the new UK Supreme Court**
>
> - Concerns over the incomplete separation of powers — or 'fusion of powers' — present in the UK system; specifically, the various roles held by the Lord Chancellor and the presence of the Law Lords in the Upper Chamber of the legislature
> - Criticisms of the opaque system under which senior judges such as the Law Lords were appointed
> - Confusion over the work of the Law Lords — specifically, a widespread failure to understand the distinction between the House of Lords' legislative and judicial functions

Has the UK judiciary been strengthened by the Court's creation?

That the judgements handed down by the new Court in its inaugural year were a continuation of what had gone before, as opposed to a new departure, is hardly surprising. After all, the UK Supreme Court was established not with the aim of extending judicial power, but rather in response to a number of long-standing problems (see Box 9.2).

Has the actual power of the highest level of the judiciary been 'strengthened'?

In November 2008, the soon-to-be President of the UK Supreme Court, Lord Philips, offered his thoughts on the role of the new Court in a speech to the Law Society:

> Our Supreme Court is attracting huge interest worldwide. One question that I am repeatedly asked is, 'What difference is it going to make?' In theory, it need not make much. The change is [largely] one of form rather than of substance...[but] it is plain that there are many who are hoping that the move across Parliament Square will prove a catalyst for change.

Lord Philips' comments highlighted the paradox apparent in the media coverage of the new Court, namely that a body that was to be given no new powers was nonetheless widely expected to assume a more pivotal role within the UK system.

Under the Constitutional Reform Act (CRA, 2005), the new UK Supreme Court simply took on most of those roles previously performed by the Law Lords (see Box 9.3).

Box 9.3 The powers of the UK Supreme Court

- To act as the final court of appeal in England, Wales and Northern Ireland
- To hear appeals on issues of public importance surrounding arguable points of law
- To hear appeals from civil cases in England, Wales, Northern Ireland and Scotland
- To hear appeals from criminal cases in England, Wales and Northern Ireland (with the High Court of Justiciary retaining jurisdiction over criminal cases in Scotland)

Has the independence of the senior judiciary been 'strengthened'?

Judicial independence in the UK is based upon six main pillars. To what extent has the protection afforded to judicial independence been strengthened in each of these areas?

1 **The security of tenure enjoyed by judges.** Judges are appointed for an open-ended term, limited only by the requirement that they must retire by the age of 75. This means that politicians cannot seek to bring influence to bear by threatening to sack or suspend them. It is extraordinarily hard for judges at High Court level and above (i.e. the 'senior judiciary') to be removed. Indeed, this can only take place as a result of impeachment proceedings requiring a vote in both houses of parliament. However, those in more junior ranks of the judiciary could always be removed by the Lord Chancellor and the Lord Chief Justice. For example, on 17 May 2008, the *Guardian* reported the results of a Freedom of Information Act (2000) request confirming that two junior judges had been dismissed for misconduct in 2005.

Strengthened		Unchanged	✓

2 **Guaranteed salaries paid from the Consolidated Fund.** The salaries of judges cannot be altered with the aim of putting pressure on them because control of judges' pay has been placed beyond everyday political control. As a result, judges are free to make decisions as they see fit without fear of financial penalty, and politicians are unable to offer judges financial inducements to make the decisions they want.

Strengthened		Unchanged	✓

3 **The offence of contempt of court.** Under sub judice rules, the media, ministers and other individuals are prevented from publicly speaking out during legal proceedings. This requirement is designed to ensure that justice

is administered fairly, without undue pressure being brought to bear by politicians or the public in general.

Strengthened		Unchanged	✓

4 **The separation of powers.** The downgrading of the post of Lord Chancellor and the creation of a new UK Supreme Court has enhanced the separation between the senior judiciary and the other branches of government. Prior to these changes, the most senior judges, the Law Lords, sat in the House of Lords and the Lord Chancellor held significant roles in all three branches of government: executive, legislature and judiciary.

Strengthened	✓	Unchanged	

5 **An independent appointments system.** The Constitutional Reform Act (2005) saw the creation of an independent Judicial Appointments Commission. This brought greater transparency to the process of judicial appointments and served to address concerns that the system in place previously had been open to political bias. The system used to appoint Supreme Court Justices is also said to be an improvement on the one by which Law Lords were appointed previously.

Strengthened	✓	Unchanged	

6 **The training and experience of senior judges.** Most senior judges have served an 'apprenticeship' as barristers and come to the bench having achieved a certain status within their chosen profession. It is argued that such individuals take considerable pride in their legal standing and are therefore unlikely to defer to politicians or public opinion, where this would be seen to compromise their judicial integrity. In allowing non-judges such as experienced barristers to become Supreme Court Justices, the available recruiting pool has been significantly widened and enhanced.

Strengthened	✓	Unchanged	

Has the membership of the highest court of appeal been 'strengthened'?

The UK Supreme Court consists of 12 Justices (see Table 9.1). The founding Justices of the new Supreme Court were those active Law Lords in post at the time of the move to Middlesex Guildhall on 1 October 2009. Under the Constitutional Reform Act (2005), the most senior Law Lord at that time, Lord Phillips of Worth Matravers, took on the role of President of the Court, with the second most senior, Lord Hope of Craighead, assuming the role of Deputy President.

Although these founding Justices of the Supreme Court themselves remained members of the House of Lords, they were barred from sitting and voting in the Upper Chamber for as long as they remained in the new Court. Under the Constitutional Reform Act (2005), those appointed to the Court subsequently are not automatically elevated to the Lords (as seen with the appointment of Sir John Dyson to the Court from 13 April 2010).

The Constitutional Reform Act (2005) saw control over most appointments to the senior judiciary pass into the hands of the new independent Judicial Appointments Commission (JAC). However, appointments to the UK Supreme Court operate under an entirely separate system whereby an ad-hoc independent commission nominates a single individual for confirmation by the Lord Chancellor.

Table 9.1 The composition of the UK Supreme Court in April 2010 (ranked by seniority)

	Justice	Birth date	University
1	Lord Phillips of Worth Matravers President of the Supreme Court	21/01/1938	King's College, Cambridge
2	Lord Hope of Craighead Deputy President of the Supreme Court	27/06/1938	St John's College, Cambridge University of Edinburgh
3	Lord Saville of Newdigate Justice of the Supreme Court	20/03/1936	Brasenose College, Oxford
4	Lord Rodger of Earlsferry Justice of the Supreme Court	18/09/1944	New College, Oxford University of Glasgow
5	Lord Walker of Gestingthorpe Justice of the Supreme Court	17/03/1938	Trinity College, Cambridge
6	Baroness Hale of Richmond Justice of the Supreme Court	31/03/1947	Girton College, Cambridge
7	Lord Brown of Eaton-under-Heywood Justice of the Supreme Court	09/04/1937	Worcester College, Oxford
8	Lord Mance Justice of the Supreme Court	06/06/1943	University College, Oxford
9	Lord Collins of Mapesbury Justice of the Supreme Court	07/05/1941	Downing College, Cambridge Columbia Law School, New York
10	Lord Kerr of Tonaghmore Justice of the Supreme Court	22/02/1948	Queen's University, Belfast
11	Lord Clarke of Stone-cum-Ebony Justice of the Supreme Court	13/05/1943	King's College, Cambridge
12	The Rt Hon Sir John Anthony Dyson Justice of the Supreme Court	31/07/1943	Wadham College, Oxford

How has the new appointments process worked in practice?

Though one would hardly expect a superior court such as the UK Supreme Court to be socially representative of the broader population, the membership of the Court in April 2010 left it open to accusations of elitism: 11 of the 12 Justices had attended Oxford or Cambridge; ten had attended independent secondary schools; 11 were men; the 12 Justices had an average age of a shade under 67 years.

One of the central aims in establishing the new system of appointments to the Court had been to widen the available recruiting pool. While it was clearly inevitable that the fledgling Court would consist largely of Lords and those who had previously served at the Court of Appeal — not least because 11 of the 12 founding members made the move from the Lords in October 2009 — the system allowed for the appointment not only of sitting judges but also of senior barristers.

At the time the Supreme Court opened for business on 1 October 2009, it only numbered 11 Justices, rather than the 12 provided for in law. This was because one of the 12 Law Lords, Lord Neuberger of Abbotsbury, had accepted the position of Master of the Rolls in preference to joining his fellow Law Lords in the new Court.

Although the resultant vacancy was eventually filled by Sir John Dyson, a candidate of obvious merit, the process that led to Dyson's confirmation provoked far more controversy than might have been expected. At one stage it appeared likely that Dyson, a serving judge on the Court of Appeal, would be overlooked in favour of the part-time judge and eminent QC Jonathan Sumption. Indeed, it was even reported that the Lord Chancellor — Justice Minister Jack Straw — had indicated his willingness to confirm Sumption. However, on 4 February, the *Times* reported that Sumption had not even been shortlisted for the post in the wake of opposition from senior figures on the Court of Appeal.

All of this naturally raises serious questions regarding the degree to which the new appointments process is truly meritocratic and independent. As the *Times*' Frances Gibb commented, 'if the appointment of an outstanding outsider can be thwarted in the face of Parliament's wish to open up the judiciary, the revamped appointments process looks little more than a sham'.

Is the Court likely to have an impact on the independence and authority of the senior judiciary?

An enhanced public profile
The physical separation
The Appellate Committee of the House of Lords that acted as the highest court of appeal prior to the creation of the UK Supreme Court was, from the

public perspective at least, shrouded in mystery. As the BBC's Chris Summers noted back in 2007, 'Ask any tour guide in Washington DC and they will be able to direct you to the US Supreme Court. Make the same enquiry of a London guide about the UK version and they would be left scratching their head.' The move to Middlesex Guildhall therefore had a significance beyond simply taking the active Law Lords out of the Palace of Westminster. Giving the new Court its own building served also to raise its profile, engender greater public interest in the Court and allow it to develop a distinctive identity and character.

Demystifying the Court

The decision to have Supreme Court Justices taking to the bench without their traditional wigs and robes has gone some way towards removing the sense of otherworldliness that often surrounded the Law Lords. The likelihood of regular televised sessions should also serve to demystify the senior judiciary and might also have the effect of paving the way for a new relationship between the media and senior judges. In addition, the Court's website already carries downloadable texts of its rulings along with press summaries of many judgements. This will allow for greater public scrutiny of the workings of the Court.

Greater authority

It is likely that the changes outlined above will affect the way in which other branches of government view the new Court and their own position and power in relation to it. Though the new Court holds no more power than the Law Lords it replaced at the apex of our legal system, such changes may well serve to lend the judiciary greater legitimacy and authority.

Summary

- The process by which appointments are made to the UK Supreme Court is less opaque and more independent than that which had existed previously in respect of Law Lords.
- This new process may well affect the future composition of the Court, though there is little evidence to support this conclusion at present.
- The move across Parliament Square to Middlesex Guildhall has not been accompanied by any significant strengthening of the Court's powers.
- Though judicial independence appears to have been strengthened, with a clearer separation of powers, the friction that already existed between leading judges and politicians would suggest that the higher levels of the UK judiciary were already functionally independent.
- The public and media profile of those judges that sit at the apex of the UK judiciary has been significantly strengthened by the creation of the new Court and this is already starting to affect the way in which other branches of government act in relation to the judiciary.

Exam focus

To consolidate your knowledge of this chapter, answer the following questions:

1 What were the problems that prompted the creation of the new UK Supreme Court?
2 How far has the independence of the judiciary been strengthened by the creation of the Supreme Court?
3 To what extent is the new appointments process 'truly meritocratic and independent'?
4 To what extent has the UK judiciary been strengthened as a result of the creation of the Supreme Court?

Who's who in UK government and politics?

Cabinet		
Name	**Party**	**Post**
The Rt Hon David Cameron MP	Con	Prime Minister, First Lord of the Treasury and Minister for the Civil Service
The Rt Hon Nick Clegg MP	LD	Deputy Prime Minister, Lord President of the Council (with special responsibility for political and constitutional reform)
The Rt Hon William Hague MP	Con	First Secretary of State, Secretary of State for Foreign and Commonwealth Affairs
The Rt Hon George Osborne MP	Con	Chancellor of the Exchequer
The Rt Hon Kenneth Clarke QC MP	Con	Lord Chancellor, Secretary of State for Justice
The Rt Hon Theresa May MP	Con	Secretary of State for the Home Department and Minister for Women and Equalities
The Rt Hon Dr Liam Fox MP	Con	Secretary of State for Defence
The Rt Hon Dr Vincent Cable MP	LD	Secretary of State for Business, Innovation and Skills
The Rt Hon Iain Duncan Smith MP	Con	Secretary of State for Work and Pensions
The Rt Hon Chris Huhne MP	LD	Secretary of State for Energy and Climate Change
The Rt Hon Andrew Lansley CBE MP	Con	Secretary of State for Health
The Rt Hon Michael Gove MP	Con	Secretary of State for Education
The Rt Hon Eric Pickles MP	Con	Secretary of State for Communities and Local Government
The Rt Hon Philip Hammond MP	Con	Secretary of State for Transport
The Rt Hon Caroline Spelman MP	Con	Secretary of State for Environment, Food and Rural Affairs
The Rt Hon Andrew Mitchell MP	Con	Secretary of State for International Development
The Rt Hon Jeremy Hunt MP	Con	Secretary of State for Culture, Olympics, Media and Sport
The Rt Hon Owen Paterson MP	Con	Secretary of State for Northern Ireland

Cabinet		
Name	Party	Post
The Rt Hon Michael Moore MP	LD	Secretary of State for Scotland
The Rt Hon Cheryl Gillan MP	Con	Secretary of State for Wales
The Rt Hon Danny Alexander MP	LD	Chief Secretary to the Treasury (and providing ministerial support to the deputy prime minister)
The Rt Hon Baroness Warsi	Con	Minister without Portfolio
The Rt Hon Lord Strathclyde	Con	Leader of the House of Lords, Chancellor of the Duchy of Lancaster

Ministers also attending cabinet		
The Rt Hon Francis Maude MP	Con	Minister for the Cabinet Office, Paymaster General
The Rt Hon Oliver Letwin MP	Con	Minister of State, Cabinet Office (providing policy to the prime minister in the Cabinet Office)
The Rt Hon David Willetts MP	Con	Minister of State (Universities and Science), Department for Business, Innovation and Skills
The Rt Hon Sir George Young Bt MP	Con	Leader of the House of Commons, Lord Privy Seal
The Rt Hon Patrick McLoughlin MP	Con	Parliamentary Secretary to the Treasury and Chief Whip
The Rt Hon Dominic Grieve QC MP*	Con	Attorney General

* attends when required

Office of the prime minister (key figures)	
Ed Llewellyn	Chief of Staff
Kate Fall	Deputy Chief of Staff
Steve Hilton	Director of Strategy
Andy Coulson	Director of Communications
James O'Shaughnessy	Head of Policy Unit

Civil Service Permanent Secretaries with their responsibilities	
Jeremy Heywood	Cabinet Office (10 Downing Street)
Sir Gus O'Donnell	Cabinet Office (Cabinet Secretary and Head of the Home Civil Service)
Matt Tee	Cabinet Office (Communications)
Ian Watmore	Cabinet Office (Efficiency and Reform)
Alex Allan	Cabinet Office (Intelligence)
Sir Jon Cunliffe	Cabinet Office (International Economic Affairs and Europe)
Sir Peter Ricketts	Cabinet Office (Security)

Civil Service Permanent Secretaries with their responsibilities	
Sir Bob Kerslake	Communities and Local Government
Keir Starmer QC	Crown Prosecution Service
Martin Donnelly	Department for Business, Innovation and Skills
Jonathan Stephens	Department for Culture, Media and Sport
David Bell	Department for Education
Dame Helen Ghosh	Department for Environment, Food and Rural Affairs
Minouche Shafik	Department for International Development
Robert Devereux	Department for Transport
Sir Leigh Lewis	Department for Work and Pensions
Darra Singh	Department for Work and Pensions (Chief Executive of Jobcentre Plus)
Moira Wallace	Department of Energy and Climate Change
Una O'Brien	Department of Health
Professor Dame Sally Davies	Department of Health (Chief Medical Officer) (Interim)
Sir David Nicholson	Department of Health (NHS Chief Executive)
Simon Fraser	Foreign and Commonwealth Office
Professor Sir John Beddington	Government Chief Scientific Adviser
Iain Lobban	Government Communications Headquarters
Dave Hartnett	HM Revenue and Customs (Second Permanent Secretary)
Dame Lesley Strathie	HM Revenue and Customs
Sir Nicholas Macpherson	HM Treasury
Tom Scholar	HM Treasury (Second Permanent Secretary)
Sir David Normington	Home Office
Sir Bill Jeffrey	Ministry of Defence
Professor Mark Welland	Ministry of Defence (Chief Scientific Adviser)
Ursula Brennan	Ministry of Defence (Second Permanent Secretary)
Sir Suma Chakrabarti	Ministry of Justice
Bruce Robinson	Northern Ireland Civil Service
Stephen Laws	Office of the Parliamentary Counsel
Sir Peter Housden	Scottish Government

Shadow cabinet	
Ed Miliband	Leader of the Labour Party
Harriet Harman	Deputy Leader and Shadow Secretary of State for International Development
Alan Johnson	Shadow Chancellor of the Exchequer
Yvette Cooper	Shadow Secretary of State for Foreign and Commonwealth Affairs and Minister for Women and Equalities

Shadow cabinet

Ed Balls	Shadow Secretary of State for the Home Department
Sadiq Khan	Shadow Lord Chancellor, Secretary of State for Justice (with responsibility for political and constitutional reform)
Jim Murphy	Shadow Secretary of State for Defence
John Denham	Shadow Secretary of State for Business, Innovation and Skills
Douglas Alexander	Shadow Secretary of State for Work and Pensions
John Healey	Shadow Secretary of State for Health
Andy Burnham	Shadow Secretary of State for Education and Election Coordinator
Caroline Flint	Shadow Secretary of State for Communities and Local Government
Maria Eagle	Shadow Secretary of State for Transport
Meg Hillier	Shadow Secretary of State for Energy and Climate Change
Mary Creagh	Shadow Secretary of State for Environment, Food and Rural Affairs
Liam Byrne	Shadow Minister for the Cabinet Office
Shaun Woodward	Shadow Secretary of State for Northern Ireland
Ann McKechin	Shadow Secretary of State for Scotland
Peter Hain	Shadow Secretary of State for Wales
Ivan Lewis	Shadow Secretary of State for Culture, Media and Sport
Tessa Jowell	Shadow Minister for the Olympics
Angela Eagle	Shadow Chief Secretary to the Treasury
Rosie Winterton	Chief Whip
Hilary Benn	Shadow Leader of the House of Commons
Lord Bassam of Brighton	Lords Chief Whip
Baroness Royall of Blaisdon	Shadow Leader of the House of Lords
Baroness Scotland	Shadow Attorney-General
Tony Lloyd	Parliamentary Labour Party Chair

Also attending shadow cabinet meetings

Jon Trickett	Shadow Minister of State, Cabinet Office

Commons Speaker and Deputy Speakers

Speaker	John Bercow
Deputy Speakers	Lindsay Hoyle (Lab)
	Nigel Evans (Con)
	Dawn Primarolo (Lab)

House of Lords Speaker	
Lord Speaker	Baroness Hayman

Chairs of Commons Select Committees	
Adrian Bailey	Business, Innovation and Skills
Graham Stuart	Children, Schools and Families (Education)
Clive Betts	Communities and Local Government
John Whittingdale	Culture, Media and Sport
James Arbuthnot	Defence
Tim Yeo	Energy and Climate Change
Anne McIntosh	Environment, Food and Rural Affairs
Joan Walley	Environmental Audit
Richard Ottaway	Foreign Affairs
Stephen Dorrell	Health
Keith Vaz	Home Affairs
Malcolm Bruce	International Development
Sir Alan Beith	Justice
Laurence Robertson	Northern Ireland Affairs
Graham Allen	Political and Constitutional Reform
Greg Knight	Procedure
Margaret Hodge	Public Accounts
Bernard Jenkin	Public Administration
Andrew Miller	Science and Technology
Ian Davidson	Scottish Affairs
Louise Ellman	Transport
Andrew Tyrie	Treasury
David T. C. Davies	Welsh Affairs
Anne Begg	Work and Pensions

UK political parties holding seats at Westminster or in the European Parliament			
Party	Party leader	MPs	MEPs
Conservative Party	David Cameron	307	25
Labour Party	Ed Miliband	258	13
Liberal Democrats	Nick Clegg	57	12
Democratic Unionist Party (DUP)	Peter Robinson	8	1
Scottish National Party (SNP)	Alex Salmond	6	2
Sinn Féin	Gerry Adams	5	1
Plaid Cymru (PC)	Ieuan Wyn Jones	3	1
Social Democratic and Labour Party (SDLP)	Margaret Ritchie	3	0
Alliance Party of Northern Ireland	David Ford	1	0
Green Party of England and Wales (GPEW)	Caroline Lucas	1	2

UK political parties holding seats at Westminster or in the European Parliament			
Party	Party leader	MPs	MEPs
British National Party (BNP)	Nick Griffin	0	2
UK Independence Party (UKIP)	Nigel Farage	0	12
Ulster Unionist Party (UUP)	Tom Elliott	0	1
Independent	N/A	1	0

Heads of devolved executives	
First Minister of Scotland	Alex Salmond (SNP)
First Minister of Wales	Carwyn Jones (Labour)
First Minister and Deputy First Minister of Northern Ireland	Peter Robinson (DUP) and Martin McGuinness (Sinn Féin)
Mayor of London	Boris Johnson (Conservative)

UK Supreme Court (in order of seniority)	
President of the Supreme Court	Lord Phillips of Worth Matravers
Deputy President of the Supreme Court	Lord Hope of Craighead
Justices of the Supreme Court	Lord Saville of Newdigate
	Lord Rodger of Earlsferry
	Lord Walker of Gestingthorpe
	Baroness Hale of Richmond
	Lord Brown of Eaton-under-Heywood
	Lord Mance
	Lord Collins of Mapesbury
	Lord Kerr of Tonaghmore
	Lord Clarke of Stone-cum-Ebony
	The Rt Hon Sir John Dyson